SEO *for* 2013

&

BEYOND

∷

SEO Made Simple
For Beginners

PARTHA BHATTACHARYA

First Printing, 2013

ISBN-13: 978-1492186717
ISBN-10: 1492186716

Printed in the United States of America

DEDICATED to my mother, Saibalini Bhattacharya, whose trust in me never faltered.

As someone who always worked hard throughout her life, my mother inspires me thus:

Be honest. Try your best. The time isn't far when you succeed.

CONTENTS

ACKNOWLEDGMENTS

I gained a lot by studying and implementing the writings, observations and opinions of acclaimed SEO practitioners in the columns of well-known websites.

I learned that the 'learning' of SEO, indeed every other knowledge, is an ongoing process, and it *never* ceases, no matter what.

I thank my friend Tapas Chakraborti, who helped in proofreading the book, and pointed out several flaws for correction.

I also thank Tania, my daughter, a columnist for Gulf News, who inspired and instilled confidence in me, that I can write a book if I want to and that my knowledge, howsoever incomplete I consider, has value for others who need it.

INTRODUCTION

S EO – or Search Engine Optimization – as we know has undergone paradigm changes many times over in the past years. This has happened and continues to happen because the search engines change their algorithms – the computer programs that auto-decide the rankings of the webpages in the search results – with the objective of *improving the user experience.*

The question is why does improving user experience become necessary if one has happened only a while back? And indeed, what does that mean for small websites?

Questions such as these are intriguing, and in fact only the companies that run the search engines like Google can properly answer them.

We can however safely conclude that the factors determining the rank-ability of webpages are to a large extent dynamic. And in such circumstances the ideal step for the small websites is to stick to the time-tested golden rules of SEO.

SEO helps when a website is focused and effective in conveying to the search bots what the site is about. On a broader perspective, SEO, contrary to popular belief, is not only about ranking well in the search engine results pages (SERPs), but is also about guiding the human visitors to get the most after they land up in a website.

How This Book Helps

Charting a new direction, this book explains the basic concepts of search engine optimization. It doesn't simply say what steps to take, but also why to take them.

Accordingly, as you'll find in the book, there is a good amount of discussions on how to focus more on structure, presentation, and quality of the contents in a website such that it attracts and retains human visitors for maximizing benefits.

Conscious efforts have gone to make this book as jargon-free as possible. Tech-heavy concepts have been carefully avoided to make it simple for a small website owner to clearly understand the actual steps he needs to take.

Separating the wheat from the chaff, this book gives plenty of examples to grasp the bigger picture of what SEO is about today, and how you can successfully use it for your web business.

To better explain the different SEO concepts nearly 170 useful articles and resources have been referred to throughout this book. The chapter-wise references are indicated by numerical superscripts, and are mentioned at the end of the book to help readers benefit from them.

Who Should Buy This Book

This book is intended for self-supported rookies and beginners who want to start a web business and need to know and implement SEO strategies from the ground up. This book will also help those who wish to take up SEO as their career either in the employment of other companies or as self-employed professionals.

Nearly all the steps described in this book can be done without incurring cost. But then, you perhaps cannot, as a website owner, do everything yourself because you have your business to look after.

The question of spending money for your website comes only when you decide to outsource some of the works so that you can devote quality time for your business.

Special Bonus

I have included a special bonus for the readers of this book. As a reader, you will get lifetime access to my video-based e-learning course, *SEO Best Practices for Beginners to Start Web Business*, at Udemy, the online education portal of repute.

This well-explained popular course costs $45 but it comes free to the readers, and the coupon code for free access is available later inside this book.

How to Contact the Author

Your views are most welcome. Feel free to contact me at my email address, *team@hubskills.com.*

You may also reach me by visiting my website, *http://hubskills.com/* and filling in the contact form there.

SEO *for* 2013

&

BEYOND

::

SEO Made Simple
For Beginners

1

UNDERSTANDING SEARCH ENGINES

S earch engines have special software robots, often called crawlers, whose main job is to locate and build a list of words they find in the websites they go through. The crawlers usually start from popular web pages and heavily used servers, and follow all the links there to spread all over the web.

See the following image (Figure 1.1), created after the illustration in *HowStuffWorks*[1.1].

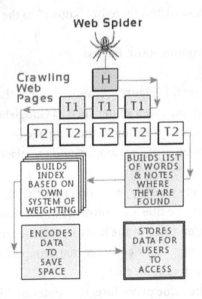

Figure 1.1

When search engine crawlers like Google's *Googlebot* visits a webpage, they usually record *2 sets of vital information from the page*:

- Individual words within the page and how frequent are their occurrences, and
- Where the words are located in the page HTML.

Words that occur in the title tag, other meta tags, and in other special places in the page convey their relative importance in that page.

They are noted by the crawler and the concerned page is later considered for listing following a search query for one or more of those relevant words.

Remember that in order to have your website's pages crawled, they must be 'found'. This means that at least one page in your website must be linked from another web page that has already been crawled and therefore 'known' to the search engine.

How Search Engines Rank Pages

In the above diagram (Figure 1.1) notice that at the time of crawling a webpage, a web spider such as Googlebot builds a list of important words appearing in the webpage (excepting 'a', 'an', 'the'), their frequency of appearance, and the places where they occur.

When the same word or more precisely the same group of words appears in the title and sub-titles of the page, in the meta description tag, and also in the body text of the page, the crawling spider may likely consider that group of words as important and relevant for that page.

Following the same procedure, the spider builds an index of relevant words for the webpage based on its own 'system of weighting'.

In a similar way, the indexing is done for other pages in the website and for all the billions of webpages that are crawled by the search engine spiders.

Finally, the spider encodes the indexed data and stores them securely in another place. This entire cycle of events by the search engine spider goes on non-stop every single moment of every single day.

All search engines have their proprietary, closely-guarded set of rules that determine how much 'weight' to give to a webpage with respect to its relevance for a certain word or a group of words. *This set of rules is popularly called an algorithm.* The algorithm is changed by the search engine owner as and when it feels necessary to do.

When a surfer looks for information for a search term, the search engine immediately dips into the huge mass of encoded storage data, and then fetches the webpages considered the most relevant for the search term in the list of results.

In actuality, the relevance of a webpage vis-à-vis a search term is not dependent on the word indexing only as explained above.

There are other crucial factors that play much bigger roles, like the structure of the website, relevance and spread of contents, quality of incoming links, internal linking, site speed, and so on.

Find out what Google has to say about its algorithms that *rank relevant results higher*[1.2].

What Happens When Search Engine Algorithm Changes

As evident, the listing of relevant webpages in the search results for a particular search term is completely controlled by the algorithm of the respective search engine. Therefore, if there is a change in the algorithm either by design or accident (mainly by design), the list of search results may also change as well.

Usually, the change in algorithm occurs when the search engine wants to update the indexing process. This is necessary for the search engines because they will want to have the most relevant search results presented to the user every time he does a search for his chosen search term.

A simple explanation for an algorithm change can be that when the search engine tests the results for each probable search term it has in its massive repository and finds that there is scope for improvement in the final results in terms of a new set of parameters, it may tweak the algorithm to reflect that.

If you look at the Google Algorithm Change History maintained by Moz[1.3], there already have been 7 major changes in 2013 so far after roughly 38 changes in the previous year, 2012.

The recently started MozCast[1.4] is what it says *a weather report showing turbulence in the Google algorithm. The hotter and stormier the weather the more Google's rankings changed.*

From the viewpoint of a small website owner, the change in search engine algorithm is too tech-heavy and distracting to spend time on and be bothered about.

What Is Search Engine Optimization

Search engine optimization, or SEO, its acronym, is the aggregate of all actions that you do to your website as a whole and to all the pages within the site seeking to improve the ranking of the pages in your website in the search engine results.

In practical terms, SEO is a marketing exercise that complements your other marketing efforts with 2 clear objectives:

1. How to bring in visitors to your site from the search engine results, and
2. How to convert the visitors who come to your site

If you have a product or service to sell in your website, you are likely to employ one or more of several marketing methods like, ads, banners, sponsoring events, free offers, etc.

However, look closely and you'll find that the role of all of these marketing methods ends after bringing the visitors to your website.

In sharp contrast, the role of SEO is not only to bring visitors from the search results, but continue thereafter to retain and convert them as well.

In this larger role for SEO, there is a paramount need for creating quality and relevant website contents, since it is the contents that attract and retain the visitors in a website.

If the visitors spend more time in a website it is a signal that the contents in the site are liked by them. And when that happens, there is greater chance of converting the visitors to take some kind of action.

Coming to the core of SEO, the issue is how important and relevant a webpage is with respect to a particular set of words, called 'keywords', in the eyes of search engines.

To give an example, if the homepage of your website is considered important by Google for the keywords (or key-phrase) 'online video', then it has a good chance to rank among the top 10 search results for that search term.

Should that occur…there could be a huge surge in traffic to the homepage, giving you the opportunity to boost your web business.

It is evident that SEO encompasses a wide range of activities, all of which have to work in tandem for the best results.

At the very least some important SEO actions are as under:

1. Keyword research
2. Planning site structure
3. Website designing
4. Content development
5. Link building
6. Traffic monitoring
7. Avoiding technical glitches

As against the above, there are some techniques that seek to artificially inflate the relevance of web pages in the eyes of search engines so as to attain higher rankings in the search results.

These are known as *spamdexing* or Black Hat SEO.

3 such common techniques are:

1. Keyword Stuffing
2. Article Spinning
3. Link Farming

The point to note is that *spamdexing* never serves any good purpose in the long term. They really don't work nowadays. In fact, search engines like Google are sophisticated enough to locate such attempts in a short time. When that happens, the concerned website is punished to oblivion.

Knowing Google

Google, as we all know, is the largest search engine on the planet. Many of us use Google to search the information we want. For quite some time, it has maintained vice-like grip on search market share, owning as much as two-thirds of the total daily searches in many countries.

At this point, let me briefly refer to a study[1.5] by Betsy Sparrow of Columbia University on the use of the Internet. She found that…

> *Since the advent of search engines…. our brains rely on the Internet for memory. We remember less through knowing information itself than by knowing where the information can be found.*

This means that we are relying more and more on the search engines for different information. Imagine therefore what a huge influx of users there will be to the various search engines!!

With that knowledge let's now understand how Google matters in SEO.

Google in fact is a big marketing company, and its biggest asset is the world's largest search engine. The Total Google's revenues[1.6] in the 2013 first quarter is a little over $12.9 billion, and nearly 92% ($11.9 billion) of that comes from selling ads. Now this is very important.

As a search engine owner, Google is kind of paranoid about providing the best search experience to the users so that they come back often to use Google. And this in turn increases its revenue from advertising.

As part of its quest for better earnings Google changes the algorithm frequently, maintains an army of human evaluators to check out websites, and does not hesitate to take on big companies who it feels has done wrong things for better rankings.

Main Points to Consider

From the above it can be said that while Google does care about their product which is pretty obvious, what it doesn't care about is your website and your business.

This may sound harsh, but this is the reality.

In other words, your business may be the best of its type, but as long as it doesn't fit into Google's ways of doing things, your website hardly matters to them.

The web is huge, and considering that most traffic originate from the search results, as a small business owner the best roadmap for you will be to do things that work.

Here are some main points to consider and adhere to:

1. *Stick to proven SEO techniques.*
2. There is no shortcut to SEO.
3. *SEO is sum-total of long-drawn & continuous efforts.*
4. SEO seeks to level the field between the mightiest & the weakest.
5. Don't try unethical means…they don't succeed.
6. Don't pay heed to every expert view.
7. Find out real SEO experts and follow their views as they do many empirical research & interacts frequently.

I have *italicized* the first and the third points, because in my view they are crucial for achieving success from SEO for your web business.

2

PLANNING SEO FOR YOUR WEB BUSINESS

Understanding Your Web Business

For the sake of brevity, let me consider that your web business is one that has one or more websites meant to bring in web traffic in order to sustain and grow your business. A web business can be fully online where all the transfers of goods/services/money happen on the web with no involvement of any physical delivery.

There can also be partially-online web business where requirements are conveyed on the web, but the order fulfillment is done by actual delivery of goods or services.

In this case, the exchange of money can take place either on the web (e.g. buying a book as in Amazon's website), or physically (e.g. cash-on-delivery orders as in eBay auctions). In either case the website has to play the important role to attract and retain visitors, many of whom may convert to paying customers.

Prof Michael Rappa of the North Carolina State University has in this article[2.1] listed 9 basic categories of business models on the web. He says,

> *In the most basic sense, a business model is the method of doing business by which a company can sustain itself -- that*

is, generate revenue. The business model spells out how a company makes money by specifying where it is positioned in the value chain.

The 9 web business models according to him are:

1. Brokerage
2. Advertising
3. Infomediary
4. Merchant
5. Manufacturer (Direct)
6. Affiliate
7. Community
8. Subscription
9. Utility

Each business model has many sub-categories. For example, the Merchant model has 4 categories under it – Virtual Merchant, Catalog Merchant, Click and Mortar, and Bit Vendor.

One of these in the long list will likely be the one similar to your web business.

Though Prof Rappa's list is essentially US-based, the same concept will to a large extent apply elsewhere too.

Essentially then the first steps are to know:

1. the nature of your web business, so that you know
2. who your target customers are, and
3. how you plan to approach them.

When you have the answers to these 3 questions it will be easier to plan and structure your website in details.

What Really Matters

Like any brick and mortar business, your web business has to have a proper identity of its own. This is the most basic of all the planning you do for your web business.

An average visitor to your website should at the first glance know what your business is about.

Many people believe that once your business has a website, it will succeed. This is not true, and if you apply your mind for a while you'll realize it is not true. Let me explain.

Let us suppose that by merely having a website your business succeeds. In that case other businesses – your competitors – can and will follow the same method since making a website is so easy these days.

Eventually, in a short time you'll discover that the visitors' 'attention span' you are targeting is cluttered with many players, each vying for the same pie as you.

Evidently therefore, just to have a website does nothing to help your business unless you do something to your website that makes it get noticed in the clutter, thereby attracting larger share of eyeballs among interested web visitors.

For this to happen, your website needs to stand out amid the crowd of competition. How can you do this?

An easy way can be if you announce a 'gift for visit' scheme for your website. You will likely get lots of visitors in a short time to your website.

Many of them will come only for the gift, with scant attention for the rest of your website. In the end you may find you've given away much more compared to what you've gained from the scheme.

Well, there has to be better ways to get 'qualified' traffic to your website. We'll come to more specifics later in the book, but suffice it to say that a major factor in the success of your web business is how well your website is optimized for both the visitors and the search engines.

Connecting Business with SEO

SEO – we discussed before – is one of the ways to market your website. Very well! But pray consider...whatever would you be marketing if you don't have something to offer in your website to get something in return?

So, willy-nilly, it is the consideration for business that you want to do SEO to your website.

The consideration could be selling a product or service or collecting email addresses of the visitors who come to your website in exchange for a free e-book or something similar.

Business and SEO are kind of complementary to each other. Performance of SEO is directly related to the performance of website & performance of business. This is important. Why?

Suppose a website offers snow-jackets to the people in the desert. Do you think the business will succeed? No chance really...even if the SEO has been done well.

Then again, if a website is ugly or flash-only site, no amount of SEO is likely to help the business.

So, when is *SEO best for a business?*

Here are some indicators:

- Your product is relevant & has demand in your target market
- Your website is designed well with an eye on usability
- Your website has a system of adding fresh, targeted, relevant contents
- Your website has strategically located landing pages or squeeze pages to attract & organize flow of traffic
- Your website does not follow wrong, dubious, unproven

SEO strategy
- Your website's performances are measurable for some basic parameters
- You have patience to watch SEO work bit by bit, and acknowledge that unlike other marketing, SEO does not give results immediately
- And finally, you are ready to be in touch with the latest SEO happenings since web marketing is constantly changing.

Many of these points may not make sense right now. But they are covered later in the book.

Planning For Long Term

When I joined my first job in a large oil company in India I used to marvel at the time and effort being spent for determining the 10-years and 15-years growth strategies to be followed by the company.

I felt there was no need for this because you never really know what is going to happen 10 or 15 years hence.

I was naïve those days, and though I later realized that 10 or 15 years is perhaps too long a time to plan in advance (in some cases proving counter-productive), I also concluded that a business may turn out fragile during crisis if it doesn't have some sort of long term planning, usually for the coming 3 to 5 years.

For a web business, the long term planning will take care of the matching growth of both the business and the website so that ideally neither lags behind the other at any point in time.

According to Jeremiah Owyang[2.2], *there is a need for web strategy for every website*, and that a web strategist is responsible for the long term planning and ongoing programs for a website.

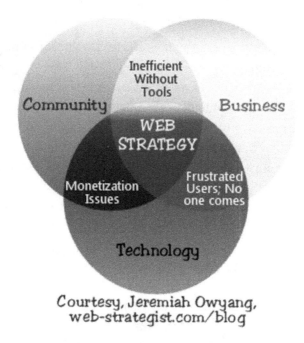

Community

Business

Inefficient
Without
Tools

WEB
STRATEGY

Monetization
Issues

Frustrated
Users; No
one comes

Technology

Courtesy, Jeremiah Owyang,
web-strategist.com/blog

Figure 2.1

Thus, the role of the web strategist will be to oversee all the 3 aspects of web business, namely community, business, and technology.

He will be more a businessman who has to seek the right balance between the 3 aspects.

For a small business, often the owner himself is the web strategist, and he has to decide the directions of both the business and the website so as to profitably run the web business.

Since he too aspires to grow big over time, there has to be some sort of planning behind all the actions he takes for his website.

A typical 1-year long-term plan for a small website could be as under (Figure 2.2).

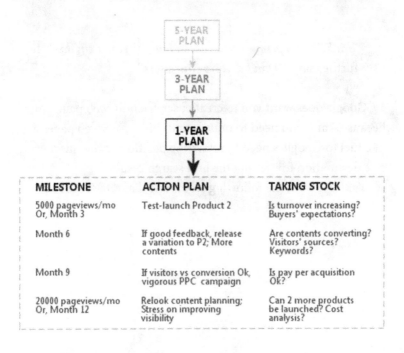

Figure 2.2

2 Main Pillars of Any Website

Consider Google as a marketing company that serves its users by providing them the best, the latest, and the most relevant results in response to their search queries.

If the results satisfy the users, they are likely to come back to Google again and again for finding more information in the future.

As a website owner your interest will be to make the site as a whole and all its pages 'friendly' in the eyes of Google.

When you do that, you increase the chance of having the pages ranked high in the search results.

How do you do that?

Interestingly, Google gives the most important advice[2,3] to the webmasters:

"Make pages primarily for users, not for search engines". It further says, *"Don't deceive your users"*.

Google does want you to create user-friendly web pages, because – and you need to understand this – your web pages are like fuel to Google's need to retain the position as the number one destination for getting the best search results.

Take a look at the following schematic diagram (Figure 2.3).

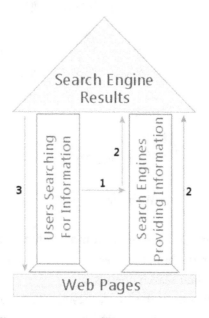

Figure 2.3

The 4 actions shown above are as under:

1
User looks for info using a search term.

2

Search engine directs user to relevant search results.

3

User clicks on a search result and goes to the webpage.

4

Going back to step 1, if user is satisfied with the webpage, he uses the search engine again for other terms.

The 2 pillars – users and search engines – are shown in perfect balance between the web pages and the search results.

This means there is no difference between what users and search engines see at a webpage.

Suppose now the webpage has too many keywords clogging the body text. When a user reads that he will be immediately put off by the excessive usage of the keyword and will likely leave the page in disgust.

Taking a step forward, if the user finds similarly bad web pages when he clicks on the other search results, he may develop a poor impression about the search engine he is using.

Consequently, he may stop using the search engine for future needs.

Obviously, no search engine wants that, and so it is in their interest that the web pages they rank at the top are really helpful for the users.

At the other end, suppose the webpage is really helpful and contains wealth of information. But it does not have a title, nor any meta description, nor a meaningful heading, nor any easily identifiable keyword.

When this happens, the search engines cannot recognize what keyword should the webpage be indexed for, and so it fails to bring this webpage in the top search results.

To conclude, ensure your webpage has all those indicators like a proper title, description, and a heading, each with the main keyword for that page. The body text may have a sparse sprinkling of the keyword.

Stop excessive usage of the keyword. Also do not take recourse to any technique that seeks to befool the readers or the search engines.

You will likely not succeed that way in the long run.

What Is a Keyword

There are many ways to define a keyword, or key-phrase, if you may. From the perspective of a user, a key-phrase is actually a search-term he is using to look for information.

At the other end, when you as a webmaster are using a particular set of words more often in the contents of a webpage, then that set of words becomes the keyword or the key-phrase for that webpage.

The question is why would you do that?

As explained in the previous chapter, all the actions of the search engines – from indexing webpages to ranking them in the search results – are done automatically by robots.

It is true that the robots are controlled by the software programs or algorithms created by humans, but after these programs are put to action, the work is automated by the robots.

For that reason the necessity of using keywords arises so that (in absence of human intervention) the search robots can identify their importance in a particular webpage, and index the page accordingly.

Consider now the importance of keywords from another angle. Let's say your webpage is about automatic monitoring of blood pressure.

Let's also suppose you are not aware that the most popular search term used by the searchers is 'automatic blood pressure monitor'.

In such a scenario, you may be using other keywords like say, blood pressure measurement, automatic blood pressure measuring, etc.

But these keywords will not bring enough traffic because they are not the ones used by the searchers.

In short, keywords are important for 3 reasons:

1. They are the ones actually used by the searchers

2. They help search engines identify the nature of the webpages and the website

3. They help establish the rank-ability of the pages, and also the authority, reputation, and brand value of a website over a long period of time

7 Features of Keywords

There are 7 core features of keywords with regard to their use in webpages and what they seek to convey to the search robots:

1. Keywords are a combination of words that are used more frequently in a webpage than any other combination of words.

2. Keywords are used in strategic places in a web page, such as the title, description meta-tag, heading, body, alt tags of images, and in one or two hyperlinks that lead to other pages.

3. The keywords must be relevant to the topic of the webpage in particular, and to the website in general.

4. The keywords are expected to be bolded or italicized at one or 2 places to mark them out when a visitor sees the page, and also for the search engines to take note of.

5. The use of keywords in various combinations in several pages over time should be able to define the reputation and authority of a website on its niche topic.

6. Keywords in a page are those that are used by other pages in your website and other websites to link to that page.

7. Finally, and the most important of all, the keywords must be those that are actually searched by the users to find information on the web.

Understanding Visitor Intent & What You Can Do

In April 2008, a team of 3 researchers led by Jim Jansen, the then assistant professor in Penn State's College of Information Sciences and Technology, analyzed more than 1.5 million queries from hundreds of thousands of search engines users.

Their findings showed[2.4] that about 80 percent of queries are informational and about 10 percent each are for navigational and transactional purposes.

Thus it can be argued that 80% of the web visitors are purely stop-and-go types, meaning they do not likely have a specific purpose in mind.

The balance 20% - shared equally between navigational and transactional types – are much more specific, and these are the visitors more likely to bring business to the website.

To give an example, the search for the term Panama is too generic. It is not clear what the user is actually looking for.

In contrast the terms '*Panama holidays*' and '*buy Panama*

holidays' clearly indicate what the user wants to know.

These are the navigational and transactional search queries respectively. Look at the image below (Figure 2.4).

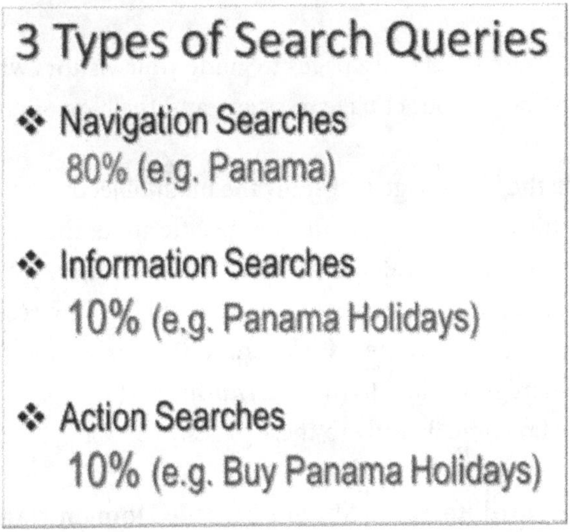

3 Types of Search Queries

❖ Navigation Searches
80% (e.g. Panama)

❖ Information Searches
10% (e.g. Panama Holidays)

❖ Action Searches
10% (e.g. Buy Panama Holidays)

Figure 2.4

Notice the differences.

When a visitor types in Panama, she is not sure what to expect from the results. However if she types in '*Panama holidays*', she is narrowing down her search.

At this stage she can be said to be interested in buying Panama holidays, but perhaps she just wants to gather information.

Finally, when she types in '*buy Panama holidays*', her intention is absolutely clear. Some experts call this type of searches as *wallet-out keywords*. This means the searcher is on the verge of making a transaction.

It is therefore obvious that a business related website has to account for the 20% of the searches that are informational and transactional in nature.

In other words, if you are selling a product or service in your website, then you have to mainly focus on how to attract and retain the 20% visitors that are informational or transactional in nature.

In that case the 3 main pages to guide your visitors will be the home page, the product page or pages, and the blog or content pages.

While the homepage will show the main objective of your website, the product pages must be specific about the items you are selling with clear calls-to-action.

It is a good idea to start a blog which will be like a reservoir where you build up contents relevant to your products. And the purpose here is 3-fold – to *inform*, *educate* and *engage* the visitors who come directly to these pages.

Why Keyword Research Should Precede Domain Name Selection

All too often when a website is thought, there is a rush to select a domain name before any meaningful planning has been made for the site.

And in many such instances, the focus quickly shifts away from what actually needs to be done, which is not a welcome sign for a new website.

Ideally when you plan a new website, your first concern will be to find out whether the product or service you want to offer in your website has enough demand in your target market.

This requires researching keywords related to your product or service, because keywords are the bridge between your website and the web to connect with the prospective visitors.

A list of important points to consider for a startup website is as under:

1. When you plan a website, find out if your product or service has enough demand.

2. To know the demand of your product or service, find out the relevant keywords that best describe your product or service, and see how popular those keywords are.

3. If your chosen keywords are highly popular, go finer and choose niche keywords for your website. For example, if 'resume writing' is a popular keyword, it is better to opt for niche keywords like 'resume writing for stay at home moms' or 'resume writing for government jobs', etc.

4. Depending upon what keywords you finally choose, re-plan your website accordingly. Your product or service will also have to be modified in line with your chosen keywords.

5. After this stage is over, and you know you have one or more profitable niches to cater for your business, the next job will be to look for suitable domain name for your website.

In the next chapter (Chapter 3) we will look at some of the ways of doing keyword research.

How to Find the Right Domain Name

It is always tricky to choose the most appropriate domain name for your web business (note I use 'web business', and not 'website'). Should you go for catchy phrases (like *google, yahoo, ebay, amazon, paypal*, etc.), or prefer one that has primary keywords in it (like *seobook, searchenginewatch*, etc.)?

If you own a well-known existing brand your task is easy. The domain name can be the brand name. If this is not the case, then selecting a domain name can indeed be a difficult job.

Let us look at some popular beliefs among website owners.

1
Belief Number One -

Having keywords as domain name does not help! I beg to disagree. You may say search engines give no special favor to keywords in domain name. Perhaps this is true!

However, having keywords in domain name *certainly helps visitors*. It is easy for a lay visitor to understand what to expect in say *jewelrydesign.com* than in *jdesign.com*. Don't you think so?

2
Belief Number Two -

Many believe that company name should be the domain name because that helps to build a brand. They are awfully wrong! Yes, if your company is Unilever or Wal-Mart or Nike or Sony, then you certainly don't need a different domain name.

But if you plan to start now or have a company that is just about a year old, it makes less sense to go for company-specific domain name. Brand comes after a business is built, not the other way round.

With that in perspective, here are some points to consider for domain naming:

1. When starting a new website/web business, a short and memorable domain name is preferable. If you can manage to get a domain with your primary keyword in it, and still a short one, it is better.

2. If you own a well-known brand name, you may still want a highly relevant domain that doesn't carry the brand name.

3. Some excellent websites that help in researching domain names are *GoDaddy.Com, DomainSamurai.Com, NameBoy.Com, DomainTools.Com,* etc.
   A couple of sleek clever tools are *DomainTyper.Com* and *Domai.nr.* A unique service from *NameChk.Com* tells you availability of your selected domain in different social networking sites.

4. If you have deep pockets you may want to buy a website, if only for the domain name.
   Try out *Flippa.Com,* a great marketplace for buying and selling domain names and websites. Watch the geographic location/influence of the domain name you may consider buying.

Often, if you have an established business, you may want the same name for your business and the web domain.

This can be a good decision, but the trouble is you may not get the domain name you want because it is already taken by someone else.

In that case you may have to compromise by either changing the domain name to something less desirable, or giving different names to the business and the domain.

In this connection take a look at the article, *How to Name Your Business*[2.5], where the author charts out 5 steps of doing it:

1. Put It in Black and White
2. Consider Your Business Structure
3. Brainstorm
4. Check for Availability
5. Register It

Structuring Your Website

A website is like a big tree with the root being its homepage. As you work with your website, you'll discover that the maximum weightage in terms of *PageRank* usually belongs to the homepage.

The homepage is connected to all the webpages in stages, which is akin to a big city that has tentacles connected to distant suburbs.

The strength of a website depends on how well it is structured.

When the website grows to thousands of pages, it can still be astutely managed if it is planned well.

At the core of it, structuring a website is about knowing how its different arms will eventually branch out as more and more pages pile up.

It's about identifying the likely future course of web business with the option for course correction midway if any such situation arises.

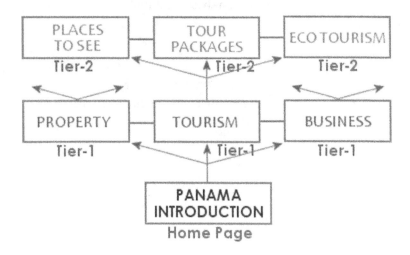

Figure 2.5

Let me take an imaginary example above (Figure 2.5), which is about the small Central American country Panama, which has the vital Panama Canal, connecting the Atlantic with the Pacific Ocean.

Let's say the main business of the website is to sell tour packages to the visitors from other countries.

Let's also suppose that the owner of the business finds out in a survey that there could be many tourists who'd like to buy properties in the island, and there will be others who'd like start a business in view of the massive expansion project of the Panama Canal.

So the website may have 3 Tier-1 pages to begin with – *property*, *tourism*, and *business*. There can be more as the business expands.

The homepage will touch upon the main direction of the website depending on the type of your web business (refer the section, *Understanding Your Web Business*). In this case it will be about selling tour packages for different segments of visitors.

Each Tier-1 page will concern about a separate aspect under the overall aegis of the web business. Tier-2 pages will thereafter take off for each Tier-1 page.

In this example, the Tier-2 pages for tourism could be places to see, tour packages, and eco-tourism. Again, there can be more Tier-2 pages as the situation evolves.

There, as you can see, the website is structured in such a way that by adding contents it can expand at Tier-2 level, and also at Tier-1 level without letting the structure go awry.

Admittedly, content planning and development need skills and good understanding of the web business. Usually the practice is to have just a few mandatory pages like About, Contact, Main Product, in your website, and have a blog and a forum.

Both the blog and the forum can have endless pages. While

you as the web business owner write a great deal about your product in the blog, your customers and visitors can use the forum extensively to speak out their minds.

Using WordPress

Since I wrote about blog in the previous section, it is perhaps natural that I extend my thought on that. WordPress is an ideal solution for growing your contents in an organized manner.

It is an open-source Content Management System (CMS), powered by PHP, a scripting language, and MySQL, a relational database management system (RDBMS).

WordPress is arguably the most popular blog software on the web that makes it very easy to add contents like text, image, video, audio, etc.

There are 2 ways you can use WordPress. Let WordPress host your blog, or you host your own WordPress blog.

If you are hosting the blog yourself, you have to hire the services of a web host, and then install WordPress in the space provided to you.

It is not difficult to do, and most web hosts have detail guide to help you start your blog.

Other than the fact that you can grow your website content almost ad infinitum, there are some compelling reasons why you may want to use WordPress for your web business site.

1. Free themes or web designs are available in plenty. WordPress has more than a thousand free themes for use in its directory[2.6], suitable for almost every conceivable web business.
   What's more, you can change the theme you choose any which way you want (if you know a bit of HTML coding), or go for a different theme any time. No need to pay a web

designer that often costs heaven.

2. Easily assign nested, multiple categories to articles, get clean permalinks for the articles, use tags for the posts, and so on. All of these go to make a well-organized content structure for your website, which is very good from the SEO viewpoint.
    In fact in a 2009 presentation Google's Matt Cutts spoke eloquently about using WordPress[2.7].

3. The most clinching factor in favor of WordPress is the rich plugin architecture that lets you do so many things in your blog. Check out for yourself some 10,000 of them in the *WordPress Plugin Directory*[2.8].

Words of caution:

If you are new to it, you may feel overwhelmed by the reach and power of WordPress, and that may result into indecision and possibly inaction. Remember, you only need to stick to the essentials, and not try out too many things at a time. Because at the end of the day it is your web business that is important and WordPress is just a tool in that process. I recommend watching WordPress tutorial videos on YouTube for any troubleshooting. Also there is a large collection of tutorials videos available at the website, *WordPress.tv*.

Growth of Website in Tandem with Growth in Business

This is a very important aspect of SEO vis-à-vis your web business. When small businesses start prospering, they soon come across a strange dilemma.
    Should they attend to the rush of prospects, or should they

first put the fledgling business on a solid foundation?

The easy answer will be to attend the ever-growing prospects. But wait.

In doing so, isn't the business owner spreading himself too thin?

In most cases this is what happens. In the pursuit of more and more business, a small business gets crippled bit by bit unless the day comes when it closes down altogether.

This happens because the small web business continues to deprive itself of the need to strengthen the foundation on which to let it sustain and flourish.

To do that it will need long-term planning, and going by the 80-20 rule made famous by the Italian economist Vilfredo Pareto, require concentrating only on those that give the most business.

In his famous 2 million copy bestseller, *The E-Myth Revisited: Why Most Small Businesses Don't Work and What to Do About It*[2.9], Michael Gerber stressed on the need to make distinction between working on your business and working in your business.

The link between web business and website will appear obvious if the latter brings in the majority of your prospects.

Even in such cases, when it is clear that you need to keep your website well-attended and updated, the circumstances may lead you to neglect your website in order to garner more business.

On the other hand, if the website is the source of a few customers, or if your business is going through a rough patch, there may be a tendency to overlook the needs of proper grooming of your website.

After all, you may wonder, what difference does it make?

But difference it does make, at least in the way the search engines look at your website.

If the website's growth lacks the vitality of frequent updating relevant to your business even when it is sort of languishing, the web business is bound to suffer as time passes.

PARTHA BHATTACHARYA

3

RESEARCHING KEYWORDS FOR
YOUR BUSINESS

We come to the most important part of search engine optimization. Knowing the search term that people use to find the information on the web is pivotal to all the actions you take to make your site's pages rank high in search results.

In the previous chapter I have briefly touched upon the fact that if your webpages do not have the KEY-phrases that people type in to look for information, then even Google cannot help you in any way.

All the quests for search engine traffic ultimately boil down to just one thing – knowing the 'popular' keywords for your business.

The emphasis is on *keywords for business*, and not website. The difference is just an indication of the approach you ought to take in this important work.

Keyword research should in fact come right at the beginning of planning a website for your business. In this chapter we will look at some of the tools that tell you the keywords people mostly use.

The emphasis is on free keyword tools, because frankly you may not need paid tools for your requirements, till at least your business grows really big.

I am not suggesting you should not pay for the paid tools, but for a small enterprise, the free tools give enough information to act on and you may not need the paid tools right away.

There are about 7 free tools discussed in the following pages, of which 3-4 are from Google's stable. They are together, in my opinion, quite formidable to start a small website on the path of keyword research for search engine optimization.

Okay, let me dive straightaway to discuss the fact that the number of words per search term is increasing, and know the reasons behind it.

Words per Search Have Increased

In the township close to where I stay there were once just a few houses, a post office, and surprisingly, a public laundry.

Whoever used to come those days to the place would inevitably be directed to their destinations with respect to the 2 easily identifiable landmarks, the post office and the laundry.

Today the township is a concrete jungle. No one remembers where the laundry is, and the post office too has remained a small entity. Each house has now its own address (as it should be), and the lanes and the roads have names for easy identification.

Whoever goes there now, search houses by their addresses, but there are a few exceptions. Some houses are found easily with respect to new landmarks, like the building next to the one with glass façade and a red top, or the building 2 lanes behind the supermarket, or suchlike.

The web reflects a similar scenario. When websites were few, just one search term fetched the results one wanted.

Today, if you type a generic term like 'shop' or 'school', you'll likely be avalanched with lots of results, many of which you may not want to see.

You'll have to refine your search to make it more specific like 'medicine shop locations' or 'kindergarten schools', etc.

This evolving concept is not far-fetched as evidenced by some of the findings that confirm that the number of words per search is increasing every year.

The reasons for the increase in words per search can be explained in 2 ways.

First, as explained above, since the number of pages have increased dramatically, searchers are learning to refine their queries to the extent they feel feasible.

Why, I often use 5 to 7 words in my search query to get the most relevant results.

The second reason is however more relevant. It ascribes the phenomenon to the contribution by Google's famed PageRank technology.

This was explained long back by Eli Goodman, comScore's Media Evangelist, who wrote[3.1]:

> *With the launching of Google's PageRank technology, incredibly relevant search results launched a revolution in both marketing and consumer behavior that has forever changed our economic and behavioral landscape. Because this technology, pioneered by Google, generated more relevant results, searchers began to feel comfortable with extending the length of their search phrases, in effect being more specific about their needs.*

Whatever the reason, the growth in words per search has continued to increase in the years.

The following graph (Figure 3.1) taken from comScore[3.2] clearly shows how between July 2008 and March 2010 the words per search in the US have grown from less than 2.9 to nearly 3.2.

The same phenomenon is reflected in the study by

WordStream[3.3] of top 20 most expensive keywords in Google AdWords advertising.

Two such expensive keywords are *'auto insurance price quotes'* and *'consolidate graduate student loans'*, both having 4 words in them.

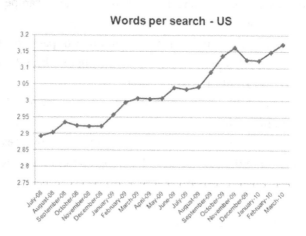

Figure 3.1

In this connection you may have to pay attention to what is referred to as the 'long tail keywords'.

The importance of long-tail keywords is explained by Google's Matt Cutts in this video[3.4].

He says:

> *…it's not temporary. This is something where we're trying to assess the quality of sites, we're trying to find the best sites that match up to long-tailed queries, and it's an algorithm change that changes how we assess which sites are the best match for long-tailed queries.*

This is a very significant change. Google has for quite a while started assessing the quality of websites in terms of long-tailed queries.

It is apparent that long-tailed queries are indicative of the spread and depth of the contents of a website. And it can be said that manipulating short keywords in a webpage in absence of quality contents does not help anymore in better rankings.

A Keyword Too Many Is Like a Red Rag

This perhaps is a no-brainer. In the next chapter I have covered the topic, *Using Keywords Naturally*, explaining how and why it is a good practice to include just a few keywords in the page copy.

Many people routinely emphasize on repeating keywords again and again in the hope that this will get the page a top rank and fetch good number of visitors. Even if that were so, don't you think the visitors will get disgusted with the page copy and leave the page in a huff?

That is indeed what happens in reality. But wait! This doesn't happen really...because of the fact that the search engines will never rank a keyword-heavy page high in search results. You guessed the reason.

Search engines won't spare any effort to eliminate all that leave bad impression with the surfers. It is their business to do so, and they do it stringently.

As mentioned in the previous section, there are lots of opportunities for you to try out long tail keywords in your page copy. And yes, do use the top keyword as well, but subtly.

Seasonality of Popular Keywords

When a major event – whether planned or unplanned – happens like the FIFA World Cup or the floods in Germany or the US presidential elections, you will find that certain related keywords are consistently figuring in the top overall searches worldwide. These search terms retain the top slots for quite a few days, sometimes even weeks or months.

Events like the ones above, or those concerning the celebrities have the potential to attract the attention of surfers worldwide, creating a spike in certain related keywords lasting for a short period. When these happen, not all websites can cash in on the opportunity, because primarily they may not be relevant to their businesses.

Another example of popular seasonal keywords can be those that are related to technology. New gadgets, new software, and suchlike dramatically alter the usage of related keywords in a short span of time.

Thus, with the release of the latest editions of gadgetry like smart phones, people increasingly search more for terms that are related to those items.

While many seasonal keywords are difficult to predict, there are some that become popular following a regular pattern. Take the example of events like the Christmas every year, or the football World Cup every 4 years.

In such cases, the keywords connected with them remain highly relevant and popular for a longer period of 3-5 months.

If your business is even remotely associated with those occasions, you must try to harness and use the likely popular keywords to cash in on the sentiments.

Keyword Relevance Vis-à-vis Your Web Business

Researching and finding the right keywords take time and good amount of effort. It is not unusual to find that the keywords that were once popular, give way to different sets of keywords as time passes.

This may happen due to improvement in technology, change

in people's perception of which keywords may likely give more relevant information.

Another reason for that is the extent of Internet usage as more people across age, gender, linguistics, and nationality start looking for information.

The change in the keyword pattern, seasonal or otherwise, may mean that the websites will also start reflecting it by way of optimizing the webpages for the changed keywords.

This may gradually result into piling up of highly optimized pages for keywords that may not properly represent the actual web business.

When this happens, it may change the course of the web business, especially if the website represents a niche business.

A friend of mine had started a website about 6 years back in which she gave her own recipes of eastern Indian foods.

She was doing well and in fact sold her recipe e-book to many interested customers. People from far beyond the Indian shores came to visit her website, and praised her efforts.

The change happened about a year back after she started writing other recipes that were not connected with the food habits of eastern India.

She says she did that because she found that the search terms for other recipes are being used in large numbers.

She shifted her priority, and since she wrote less and less about the eastern Indian foods, the number of visitors to her site also started dwindling little by little.

Fortunately, she realized fast that her web business is losing focus, and so she has of late begun to revert to her core competence once again.

She could have continued with the other recipes but she figured that it would take her a long time to establish herself in the new field.

Moreover, she would risk losing her loyal readers bit by bit, even as the tough competition in the new field would not help her getting new readers anytime soon.

Such incidents are fairly common with many web businesses. And so it is important to not go astray all of a sudden with new sets of keywords that are seemingly relevant, but in reality are not.

What to Look for in Keyword Research

Popularity of a keyword is not the only parameter in keyword research. The reason is simple.

With thousands (if not millions) of websites chasing the same keywords, it is well-nigh impossible to rank well for those keywords. Therefore, a second parameter becomes important to know.

This is called the *competitiveness* or *effectiveness* of the keyword. It seeks to find out the imbalance between the demand and supply of the keyword.

For example, if 10,000 users are using the search-term 'online video editing' (demand), but there is not enough supply of web pages for it, then the effectiveness of this search-term is very high.

If a keyword is highly popular and its effectiveness is less, then the next parameters to look for are how many pages have the keyword in page title, what is the average PageRank of the top-ranked pages, and so on.

To put in a nutshell, the following 4 are the minimum steps in any keyword research:

1. For a seed word – like seo, video, diet, blogging, etc. – which are the different key phrases or search terms being actually used by the searchers?

2. What are the demands or number of searches made per month for the respective key-phrases in different geographic locations?

3. What are the supply figures of web pages for each of these key-phrases? This will give the effectiveness of each key-phrase, also called *Keyword Effective Index* or KEI.

4. How many pages have the chosen key-phrase in the page URL, and page title?

When you do all the 4 steps diligently it is quite likely that you will be able to narrow down your quest to profitable keywords in your chosen niche.

There are quite a few keyword tools that can give you all these information to help you in keyword research, but nearly all the good ones do not come free.

If you don't mind paying for them, my suggestions would include Wordtracker[3.5] or Market Samurai[3.6].

Keyword Eye[3.7] is a comparatively low-cost visual keyword and competitor tool, but some of its features are more useful for an established website that has Google Analytics installed.

For beginners – especially websites with small budget – it may be a good idea to use the free online tools to find the desired keywords.

Google Trends Explore

At different times Google provided free keyword tools that helped the small website owners, but it discontinued them at regular intervals.

They include Wonder Wheel (demise in July 2011, replaced by related search terms at the bottom of search result pages), search-based keyword tool aka SKTool (demise in late 2010), Google Insights (demise in September 2012), etc.

The Google AdWords Keyword Tool, which also acted as the External Keyword Tool (for those without AdWords account) is an ideal tool, but it is now available only to AdWords account holders.

There is also the talk of new Keyword Planner being made available to AdWords accounts. Google however hasn't totally orphaned the small website owners.

Presently, as of this writing, it is offering a new avatar of Google Trends, which I rather call Trends Explore.

Figure 3.2

This is because out of 3 options – *Hot Searches, Top Charts,* and *Explore* – it is the last one that I believe is more useful for the beginners.

This has similarities with the now-withdrawn Google Insights. Take a look at the image above (Figure 3.2).

In this new Trends Explore tool you get the option to search for up to 5 terms at a time.

Once you choose the search terms, you have the option to further filter the results in terms of categories, time period, country, and the field of search.

In the field of search you have 5 options – *Web Search, Image Search, News Search, Product Search,* and *YouTube Search.* Notice that YouTube Search data is available as a separate option, and not as video search.

This may mean 2 things.

- YouTube by itself is a massive search platform, and so it demands a dedicated section for keyword results.
  As per statistics[3.8] more than 1 billion unique users visit YouTube each month. 70% of them are from outside US. YouTube is thus the second biggest search engine after Google.

- The second point is simply that YouTube is so big (Facebook comes a distant second – about 2.5 times less in terms of viewership – but it doesn't allow search information) that there is no other video website worth a separate search platform.

Coming to the example in the image above (Figure 3.2), 'seo tips' is the most popular on the web worldwide among 5 search terms, far outflanking the others, while 'seo blogging' is the least popular.

For each keyword and for each search option the Trends Explore tool provides related terms, and their popularity.

In the following image (Figure 3.3) the related terms for 'seo blogging' and their popularity are shown.

Figure 3.3

AdWords Keyword Tool Gives the Demand for Search Terms

While supply figures for the keywords are easily available by searching for them, the demand (or the number of searches per month) for these keywords are not known from the search results.

Google's *AdWords Keyword Tool* is a free tool that gives the demand figures for the search terms.

But as of this writing Google plans to discontinue the external Keyword Tool very shortly. Instead, for getting keyword ideas you need to sign in to your AdWords account, and then try *Keyword Planner.*

The AdWords Keyword Tool (aka *Keyword Tool External*[3.9] for those not logged in to AdWords account) offers a snapshot of important factors for the benefit of the advertisers to laser-focus their ads to the targeted customers.

To use it type in one or more search terms in the Word or phrase box – one in each line. You may keep blank or type in any website URL – even the one of your competitor – in the Website box for finding out the search terms used.

To further narrow the search criteria select the option *Category*.

Finally, the Advanced Options and Filters let you select the country for which you need the data, the language, and also the display device like computers and laptops, mobile device, etc.

If you now click the Search button you'll get a long list of keywords with respect to the selection criteria chosen by you.

The usual columns for data display are *Keyword, Competition, Global Monthly Searches, and Local Monthly Searches.*

Keyword	Competition	Global Monthly Searches	Local Monthly Searches
convert powerpoint to video ▾	Medium	40,500	8,100
powerpoint to video converter ▾	Medium	33,100	2,400
converting powerpoint to video ▾	Medium	12,100	5,400
powerpoint converter ▾	Low	201,000	18,100
powerpoint video converter ▾	Medium	33,100	2,400
convert powerpoint presentation to video ▾	Medium	2,400	880
xilisoft powerpoint to video converter ▾	Low	4,400	260
convert powerpoint to video online ▾	Medium	1,300	140
convert powerpoint to dvd ▾	Medium	2,900	1,300
convert powerpoint to video freeware ▾	Medium	2,400	170
video presentation ▾	Low	135,000	40,500

Figure 3.4

Once the data are displayed, you can further narrow down your search by opting for *Exact Match* or *Phrase Match* (by default the data are displayed for *Broad Match*) in the left pane under *Match Types*.

The image above (Figure 3.4) shows the data for Broad

Match for the term PowerPoint Video.

There are other filtering options available on the left pane allowing you to include or exclude specific terms from the keyword list.

Try out various options and combinations to get a feel of the tool. The more you do, the more you have ideas on how best you can use it for your needs.

If you are considering AdWords campaign for your products or services, or if you wish to know more about how AdWords functions, do read the help articles[3.10] provided by Google.

Benefitting From Instant Search

You may have seen that as you start typing a search term in Google's search box, you automatically get a list of terms in a dropdown.

As you continue typing the list keeps on changing depending on what you've typed thus far.

When this is happening Google also gives you a list of search results corresponding to the term typed until then.

This feature, called *Google Instant*, was introduced in September 2010 in the US, and later incorporated elsewhere.

Google has estimated[3.11] that this feature, if used by everyone globally, has the potential to shave off 3.5 billion seconds a day or 11 hours every second from the time spent on search.

Following the steps taken by Google, now other major websites like YouTube, Amazon, and eBay too have their own versions of instant search feature.

It stands to reason that the instant search feature reveals the most popular key-phrases when someone types in the words seeking information.

This is important because if you do not have the demand figures for the search terms, then perhaps instant search is a good option to choose your keywords.

The image below (Figure 3.5) shows the feature in eBay.

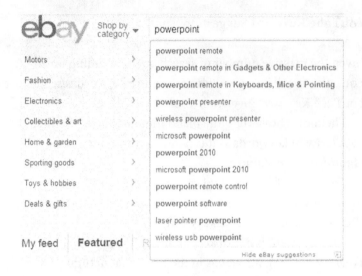

Figure 3.5

Bing Ads Intelligence (BAI)

Bing Ads Intelligence or BAI is in many respects similar to Google's AdWords Keyword Tool. You need to sign up as Bing Ads customer (even if you do not spend for the ads) to use this tool.

BAI is a powerful keyword research tool that works in Microsoft Excel 2007, 2010, or 2013. As mentioned here[3.12] the tool allows you to build and expand on your keyword lists, and enables you to easily gauge the performance of relevant keywords on the Yahoo! Bing Network.

When you use the tool, you get the lists of suggested keywords on actual Yahoo! Bing Network data, including relevance, volume, cost history, demographic, and geographic data.

Based on these rich inputs you'll be able to develop informed keyword strategies for your website and other campaigns.

YouTube Keyword Suggestion Tool

Given the massive number of search queries landing up at YouTube, it will be a good idea to explore keyword research with *YouTube Keyword Suggestion Tool*[3.13].

The tool is however quite bland though it is easy to infer popularity of keywords as it is based on just one figure, the *Monthly Search Volume.*

The results from this tool can be tailored to languages and countries that you choose, and can be based on YouTube's video URL, or one or more core keywords.

An important point to keep in mind is that people largely use YouTube looking for videos in the fields that naturally have videos, like entertainment, music, movies, sports, etc.

This means the search queries are highly skewed in favor of keywords related to those fields.

For example, when I wanted to find out the search volume for the 5 SEO-related key-phrases referred in the previous section, the YouTube keyword tool drew a blank, stating there are *Not Enough Data* available.

The best way to use YouTube as a reference for search terms is to find the keywords with instant results.

Fortunately, due to advancement in technology, the instant results option can be used in all search engines...as explained in a previous section.

Amazon Keyword Research Tool

Just as Google is the world's most popular search engine, Amazon is the world's biggest online marketplace.

Many experts feel that the keywords used in Amazon are the most relevant commercial search terms because people go to Amazon only to buy items.

Amazon's instant search feature does reveal the popular keywords. Like Google – and unlike eBay – Amazon follows the logic of *incremental search*[3.14] or real-time suggestions.

This means when a user types text, one or more possible matches for the text are found and immediately presented to the user.

In the following image (Figure 3.6), as I type the word 'powerpoint', I get 10 keyword suggestions, and all of them start with the word 'powerpoint'.

In contrast, out of 12 keyword suggestions in eBay (see Figure 3.5), there are 5 among them that do not start with the word 'powerpoint'.

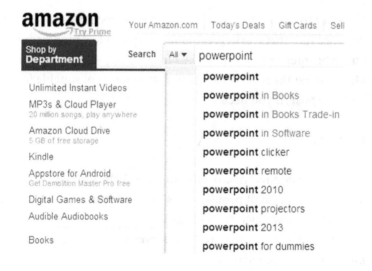

Figure 3.6

In other words, the term 'wireless powerpoint presenter' as in eBay will not come up in Amazon unless you start your search with wireless, and not powerpoint.

In spite of this shortcoming, Amazon's instant search is quite popular to ferret out relevant and useful keywords.

But you have to agree this is a painstaking, long-drawn process since you have to try out all the alphabets one by one to discover the golden nuggets you never imagined.

The importance of keyword research with Amazon cannot be overstated. A couple of keyword research tools may indeed become handy in this work.

Here they are:

1. The free tool by *Keyword Tool Dominator*[3.15], and
2. $20 worth (as of this writing) *FreshKey Keyword Analyzer Software*[3.16]

Points to Note

Keyword tools like any other software are constantly evolving. A keyword tool that works great today, may in a few months turn out to be inferior to one launched fresh. It is therefore a good idea to scout the market for the best available tool suitable for your purpose, if you decide to buy one.

Using Twitter

Twitter, the popular micro-blogging site, is the destination of a wide cross-section of people across the world, busy sending their 140-character snippets to one and all.

Twitter's catchwords are to '*discover what's happening right now, anywhere in the world*'.

And the key to unravel the trends of keyword usage is by mining the archives of tweets.

Twitter is an excellent source of instant information, but more importantly, it's an excellent source of knowing how the human minds have collectively worked in the past.

Twitter Search[3.17] is obviously the place to start looking for what all is contained inside Twitter, and finding out the combination of words used most.

For example, from the search results for the word PowerPoint I get to know that people relate it with presentation. However when I search for presentation, very few tweets mention PowerPoint.

This could mean that for many people wanting to create a presentation, PowerPoint may not be the preferred tool.

Hashtags.Org[3.18] makes an automatic record of the words in the tweets that have the symbol '#' before them.

As Twitter informs[3.19], hashtags is a Twitter community creation that has come to denote a category for different groups of tweets.

Thus, #youtube is a category called 'youtube', and it is expected that those who tweet anything about YouTube will use the hashtag #youtube in their tweets.

In practice this may not happen, and many people may not use hashtags at all. Yet, it can't be denied that the popularity of different hashtags does indicate relevance of the associated words.

This in turn is a relevant point with regard to spotting keywords for the purpose of SEO.

Übersuggest Keyword Suggestion Tool

Übersuggest[3.20] is an exciting and useful keyword tool that imitates Google Suggest and gives you a list of search terms beginning with the word or phrase you have typed.
As the site says, *Übersuggest is Google Suggest on steroids!*

Suppose you're looking for key-phrases for the term 'online'. Übersuggest will add an alphabet (a to z) or a digit (1 to 9) after 'online', and for each alphabet or digit it will extract all the keyword suggestions scraping the Google Suggest data.

There are more that can be done. Each phrase suggested by the tool can be clicked on to get further suggestions based on that phrase.

Übersuggest proclaims that

> *With the free keyword tool you can instantly get thousands of keyword ideas from real user queries! (And you can then) Use the keywords to get inspiration for your next blog post, or to optimize your PPC campaigns.*

Try the tool…you'll be pleasantly surprised.

Other Free & Paid Tools

It is likely that as a small website owner you won't need any other keyword research tool.

For your needs Google's tools may prove fairly extensive in providing information, and they do help, especially since they come from Google itself, the original custodian of the search data.

You may however want to dig in for more information as your business grows.

You may for example require elaborate keyword research for paid search marketing to exploit say seasonal demands in different demographics, or suchlike.

In such situations, when the need is to squeeze out as much information as possible including those of your competition, it is time to switch over to sophisticated paid keyword tools.

There are some paid keyword tools worth exploring. Other than *Wordtracker*[3.21] (and its newly launched Scout for Chrome browser) and *Market Samurai*[3.22] – both mentioned earlier –

WordStream[3.23] and Trellian's *Keyword Discovery*[3.24] are also popular on their individual merits.

All have their benefits, and so which one is the ideal for your needs can be known only after you have tried out all the four.

As for free keyword tool, other than those mentioned above, I'd suggest trying Aaron Wall's *SEO-Book Keyword Suggestion Tool*[3.25] that aggregates data culling from Wordtracker's basic keyword tool.

You need to open a free account to be able to use this tool.

4

KNOWING THE SEO BASICS

Designing Website That Serves

Y ou may have observed that the main Google search page is very simple, bland and ordinary, and has remained more or less the same all these years.

For Google, it's 'less is more', and for good reasons.

Let me discuss some points below to understand the issue of minimalist approach to a website design.

In *Ten things we know to be true*[4.1], Google says, "*Our homepage interface is clear and simple, and pages load instantly.*"

Earlier, Google used to maintain[4.2] that:

It aims to create designs that are useful, fast, simple, engaging, innovative, universal, profitable, beautiful, trustworthy, and personable. Achieving a harmonious balance of these ten principles is a constant challenge.

In this SEO Book article, *You Aren't Average*[4.3], the author gives the example of a survey of 50 people in New York Times Square in April 2009, wherein less than 8% knew what a browser is.

He suggests 2 very important points:

1. When designing a site, make it stupidly easy to use
2. Make the thing you do obvious

Though we are still at the beginning of this chapter, I will nevertheless ask you to read this highly relevant article, *8 Things Website Owners Can Learn From Gordon Ramsay*[4.4].

It will set the stage for your role as a search engine optimizer for your web business. Many of the issues in the article are covered in this book in due course.

I take you through these instances, coming as some of them do from none other than Google itself, to stress the 'fact' that websites with simple yet elegant designs perform better.

It is like – to take the example of Google's homepage – having only one exit in a room so that when anyone enters he just does not miss how to leave the room.

Having made the point above, let me admit that many small website owners are too eager to use every inch of the page real estate with an eye on earning more money mainly by displaying ads.

The irony is too much of ads and other contents easily distract the viewers, and that may result into their leaving the page too soon.

Hear the golden advice from Ken Evoy's SiteSell on *how to build any business online*[4.5]:

> *Web users search for information, for solutions. They are not looking for you - they don't know you (yet!). They seek what you know. Give it to them. Convert your knowledge into in-demand Content. To succeed online, start where they start - at "the search."*

Ken's suggestion is simple. He stresses on the need to follow the model, C > T > P > M, where 'M' or *Monetization* comes last.

The C, T, and P stand for *Content, Traffic*, and *Pre-Sell*. Ken says that it is the content that brings traffic, and when sufficient traffic comes, the time is ripe to pre-sell your product.

According to Ken:

> *"M" cannot happen if you fail to first execute C > T > P. This is where 99% of small businesses fail.*

If you follow the logic thus far, you may appreciate why simple yet elegant website design always serves better. As the author of the SEO Book article above says:

> *"Your website design should ask nothing more of the user than a car does. Assume nothing, other than the user will point and click something obvious."*

The key lesson is therefore to take a discerning view and strike a balance between what is really needed to be there in your website versus what can be omitted for the sake of simplicity.

Making Page Navigation Evident & Easy

Going by the underlying logic in the previous section, it will be apparent that the navigation from one page to another in your website ought to be made simple, evident and easy to notice.

This makes the job of a first-time visitor to your website simple, making him feel welcome and comfortable during his stay.

There are many ways used by the web designers to create navigation menus. In most cases, the main navigation menu is preferred at the top while those of lesser importance come on either the left or the right side. At the footer come usually those page links, like terms of use, site designer, copyright notice, etc.

You may like to use CSS or JavaScript to design the navigation menu, but using flash for the purpose is best avoided.

Images and/or buttons are also not preferable as navigating links, but if used, they should be accompanied with suitable alt tags (alt tag is explained later).

The Importance of Page Title

The page title is usually the only element that appears unchanged in the search listings.

It is the first and the only important parameter that enables a new viewer to decide whether your webpage is worth visiting and spending time in.

Page title is enclosed within the pair of title tag (<title> and </title>), and extends to about 65-72 characters depending on search engines in the search results before it is cut off.

Let us look at some points as to the importance of page title:

- Search engines use the page title as the heading of each search listing.

- When a webpage is open, the page title appears as the window title on most browsers.

- If the page is bookmarked (Ctrl+D), the page title becomes the name of the bookmark.

- When several tabs are open in a browser, then the first few words of the page title show up as the label for the tabs not being currently seen. Once again when you move the mouse on the tabs/windows that are not open, the full title floats up in a separate box.

Here are some important features for the page title (refer this article[4.6]):

1. The page title should be no more than 66 characters long.

2. It should preferably be made of one or two complete sentences.

3. Avoid using special characters like dash, colon, etc.

4. The keyword(s) of that page should be included in the page title.

5. The keyword(s) should be placed as close to the beginning as possible.

6. Attempt some sort of 'call to action' in the page title, or at least something that has the power to lure your viewers.

7. It is better to avoid the name of the website or the company in the page title, unless you are consciously building up a brand.
    For most small businesses, brand building is not usually a priority. So, keep away from wasting precious space in the page title.

8. Do not use the same page title for any 2 pages. They must be different for different pages. Search engines may not like several web pages having the same title.

9. All pages in the website – even including pages like Terms

of Use, Copyright, etc. – should have appropriate page titles.

Let me now give the example of page title of the homepage in my online video production website:

Learn Online Video Production. Make And Mix 5 Types Of Web Videos.

Check out if this page title satisfies all the features mentioned above.

Is Meta Description Necessary?

There are conflicting views on the need of meta description in the head section of your page HTML, but let us get it from the horse's mouth.

In this 2009 blog post, Google does not use the keywords meta tag in web ranking[4.7], Google's Matt Cutts lets out the following:

Even though we sometimes use the description meta tag for the snippets we show, we still don't use the description meta tag in our ranking.

That may be true but in some cases Google is likely to use the description meta tag as it is, as shown in the following example (Figure 4.1).

Figure 4.1

In other cases, for example in Google Alert, some results often show up when the chosen keyword (for sending the alerts) keyword matches with the title and also the meta description of a webpage.

If you write a blog, then the RSS feed of the posts also carry the meta description as the page description.

Looking at all these factors, let me draw the following conclusions:

- Google does not consider meta description for ranking purpose. This may presumably be because a page can likely rank for other search terms than what it is optimized for, and in that case Google will randomly select snippets from the page instead of meta description.

- Search results for the exact term that a page is optimized for may likely show the unaltered meta description.

- In the case of Google Alerts, the meta description may likely show up as the main description for the page included in the alert. In case of RSS Feed, the meta description is usually the main description for the blog posts.

It is therefore a good idea to include meta description for all the pages in a website. While doing so, the following important points may be kept in mind:

1. Most search engines usually show up to about 150-161 characters in the meta description including spaces. Anything beyond is truncated. Try to keep yours within that limit.

2. As with the page title, include the keyword phrase for that page right at the beginning of the description, say within the first 3 words.

3. Keep the meta description short, to-the-point, and possibly include some call-to-action.

4. Both the page title and the meta description should unfailingly reflect the page content. If the content differs a lot, the viewers may feel 'cheated' which is not a good thing.

The Main & The Sub Headings

Headings and subheadings visually show readers how your ideas are organized within your text. Each heading should accurately tell readers what each section covers.

The above guideline is given at the *Writing@CSU* project[4.8] of the Colorado State University. Though this guideline is for general awareness, its importance applies for a webpage also.

Headings are usually denoted by the tags H1, H2, H3, H4, H5, and H6.

As the logic goes, a page should have one main heading at the top of the page to be represented by the H1 tag (<H1>...</H1>).

This main heading sets the tone for the entire content of the page, and a surfer, having earlier seen the page title and possibly the meta description of the page in the search results, will easily understand what to expect in the page when he visits it.

While the H1 tag is used just once in a webpage for the main heading, you must use the hierarchically lower headings tags like H2 or H3 for the subheading of each group of contents, coming as they do, later in the page under the main heading.

Similar to page title and meta description, include the keyword phrase in the main heading, and preferably in sub-headings as well.

Once again, the keyword phrase in the beginning of the heading is always a good idea.

Thus, if 'online video' is my keyword phrase, then the main heading

Online Video Is The Next Big Thing

is surely better than the heading

The Next Big Thing To Hit The Internet Is Online Video.

As a reputed web marketer once said:

Headings offer important clues to the search engines... Since headlines often contain important hints to the content of the webpage, search engines take note of any keywords found here.

Using Keywords Naturally

How important is keyword for your webpage? There can be many ways to answer this question, but let us have it straight. Sage Lewis points out in this article[4.9]:

> *If you want to come up in the search engines, in the natural search results, you have to use the words your potential visitors are using to search for your company. It's just that simple. You can't come up in the search engines for phrases you don't use on your site.*

Having said that what is often misunderstood is the concept of using keyword in the body text of a page.

Figure 4.3

Undue weightage on keyword usage may lead to its overuse, rendering the content unreadable. I've tried to explain this phenomenon in the clip art shown above (Figure 4.2).

Note the 'red' in the image refers to the grey color.

As I've explained in the section, *2 Main Pillars of Any Website*, in Chapter-2 (Figure 2.3), the contents you write in a webpage are for the consumption of both the search engines and more importantly, the visitors who come to your website looking for information.

Isn't it then obvious that your page content has a judicious mix of keyword at strategic places so as to please both?

Karon Thackston, the copywriting expert, observes[4.10]:

> *It doesn't take a boatload of keyphrases shoved here, there and everywhere to make good search engine copy. In fact, that's the recipe for disaster when writing optimized text. Why? Because you have a dual audience: the search engines and, most importantly, your site visitors. Not recognizing this fact is one of the biggest mistakes made with SEO copywriting.*

What follows then is that you've to use keywords in your page copy, but you cannot afford to make it unreadable with excessive usage.

You have to use keywords naturally so that no eyebrow is raised when one reads the copy.

Let me show you an example of how cleverly Karon uses keywords in the page copy. For the keyword phrase, *discount office supplies*, here is her take:

> *Whether you're stocking up on Post-it notes or redecorating your lobby, you'll find everything you need at a deep*

discount. Office supplies, furniture, accessories and more are available at wholesale prices direct to the public. Because we buy in bulk, we pass the savings on to you through a members-only discount.

Office supplies have never been so affordable! Contact us today for complete details on joining the XYZ Office Supplies member program.

Notice that at 2 places she has used the keyword phrase split in 2 consecutive sentences, and in one case the second sentence comes in a new paragraph.

This goes to show that it is possible to write your page copy cleverly to meet the twin purpose of satisfying both the search engine and the visitor.

All of this depends on the skill of the person who writes the content.

Website owners are prone to overlook the importance of good content, stressing instead on good web design at the cost of hiring a skilled copywriter.

This is a fundamental mistake because of the simple reason that search engines rank pages in the results based on their contents, and not how the pages look like.

More on the importance of content is covered in the section, *Creating Contents That Work.*

Keyword in Page URL

There is a lot that goes in the name of SEO, and a lot that doesn't. Some concepts are debated hotly, and experts come out with opinions on either side of the fence. Keyword in page URL is one such.

Jill Whalen of HighRankings.com believes that keywords in page URL have no use. In an article of 2007 she says[4.11]:

I would highly recommend *not* changing your URLs at all. It is a common misconception that keywords in URLs are somehow helpful to search engine rankings, when in reality, they have very little (if any) effect on rankings.

Taking an opposite view, here is what Google's Matt Cutts has to say[4.12]:

Other things that we use: things in the title, things in the URL, even things that are really highlighted, like h2 tags and stuff like that. So if your blog has p=123, you are massively missing out on opportunity to put a few keywords, not keyword stuffing, just a few keywords in your URL. So Mattcutts.com/blog/samplepost -- it works pretty well. If you want to throw in the date, feel free, but make sure that you put the title and the keywords in your URL in some way.

Which of the 2 you should follow? In my considered opinion, follow Matt Cutts' advice.

It's not only that his advice is how you may expect Google looking at things. That may be a big reason. But there is a common sense to it as well.

Take the example of a blog post in Wordpress. It takes the post title automatically as the page URL. And since it is likely that the keyword for that post will be in the post title, the same is also represented in the page URL.

In his article on SEO versus SEF (search-engine-friendliness), Mark Jackson is fairly forthright. According to him[4.13]:

Not every website that has a good URL structure is search engine "optimized." A good URL structure might be defined as something that resembles this:

www.sitename.com/category/product-name/

*A poor URL structure (for search engine "friend-liness")
would be something like:*

*www.sitename.com/IWCatProductPage.process?Mer-
chant_Id=1&Section_Id=691&Product_Id=1439522&Paren
t_Id=302&default_color=BLACK&sort_by=$ioncolor=$ions
ize=*

*Yes, the above example of "bad" comes from an actual top
Internet retailer's website.*

In the design and content guidelines for webmasters, Google
does say[4.14]:

*If you decide to use dynamic pages (i.e., the URL contains a
"?" character), be aware that not every search engine spider
crawls dynamic pages as well as static pages. It helps to keep
the parameters short and the number of them few.*

So...if you include keyword in page URL, how much does it
help? Does it guarantee top rank in search result?

Well, the truth is that just one factor does not make any
significant impact in search engine ranking. It's the coming
together of many other factors that present a combined strength
to boost the chance of a webpage ranking well in the search
results.

Keyword in page URL is just one of them.

Making Content Easy To Read

Simple website design is too often felled at the altar of eagerness
to earn more money. For small website owners, there is
sometimes the overwhelming need to generate revenue from the
space in the page, and that may lead to neglecting the contents in

that page.

This is unfortunate because the search traffic comes for the page content, and not for clicking on ads present in the page.

If the viewer likes the content, and stays back for a couple of minutes more, then and then only the chance arises of his clicking on the ads in the page.

The clue to generating revenue from your webpage lies basically in increasing the stickiness of the page for the visitors so that they are sort of 'compelled' to spend more time.

This is possible by having quality content in the page (covered in the next section), and making it easy to read.

So what are the main issues to ensure easy-to-read page content? Thomson Chemmanoor in his article has spelled out *10 Common Content Usability Mistakes on a Web Page*[4.15].

Let me excerpt some of the main ones to which I've added one or two:

1. *Clear and Descriptive Heading* – Most people online just scan the text than read the entire content. So the heading or title of the page plays a major part in the content structure.

2. *Content above the Fold* – Your most important content or the content that you want your users to read should be above the fold because it is where the screen cuts off the web page. Also the chance of the reading the content below the fold is less.

3. *Consistency of the Font and Color* – All major content element of your website like heading, sub heading and content should have similar font and color.

4. *Using of Emphasis and Bold* – This should be used very carefully. Bolding and Emphasis a text is to attract attention to the user but overdoing this can kill your content and turn

the visitors away.

5. *Using Bulleted List* – This usually is a sure winner. Bulleted list attracts viewer's attention faster than without.

6. *Readability of the Content* – Readability make the page easy to read and inviting and pleasurable to the eye. Spacing (padding) of the text is very important usability issue of a website.

7. *Too Much Content* – Don't put too much of content in one page. Online visitors don't read too much of content. They want to know what you can do for them and how to contact you for their requirements.

8. *Alignment of Text* – Alignment provides the structural framework of a content design. The most common practice is to align the content text to the left.

Creating Contents That Work

It may have occurred to you that Wikipedia, the 'free encyclopedia' as the website proclaims, is usually in the top 10 most visited websites in the entire Internet.

Spare some thoughts and you'll realize that the popularity of Wikipedia is on the account of exceedingly relevant and useful contents the site contains.

Wikipedia is an exemplary example. But take any other content-heavy website, like those of the newspapers or even the article marketing sites, and you'll most likely find them heavily visited by viewers.

Talking of web content, I recall an article by Todd Friesen, *You Don't Deserve #1*[4.16]. Todd said:

So what is the secret to SEO success now? I believe it's the value-add I mentioned earlier. That gives me something to work with. It gives social media a chance for success. It gives natural link building a kick-start. It gives users a reason to bookmark the site. It gives users a reason to share the site with others. It gives you a reason to deserve to rank.

Todd's idea of value-add amounts to contents that 'honor' the time spent by a visitor to a page by giving him something worthy in return.

This can be solid, unbiased information (as in Wikipedia), or the right kind of goods or service that is expected by the visitor.

Matt Cutts of Google gives a similar advice in his article, SEO Advice: Writing useful articles that readers will love. He says as much[4.17]:

In the last week someone wrote and said "I want you to talk about SEO, and don't give me any of that crap about good content." I'm going to beg to differ.

So this is a clarion call to all small website owners about the need of good quality, relevant contents in the site.

But then, will only good content meet your SEO target?

Stoney deGeyter of Search Engine Guide doesn't think so[4.18]. He is very clear that *It Isn't Good Content Unless it's SEO'd Content.*

I hope these examples give you a fair idea about the need of quality content in your website that gives something of real value to the visitors, and at the same time signal the search engines about the relevance of the content with respect to the search terms that the visitors want information for.

Remember, having good content is not a one-off affair. It's an ongoing process, and each time you create a webpage you have to ask yourself the question, *"Does the page offer something unique to the visitors?"*

If the answer is an honest 'yes', you may feel assured that your visitors will find value in it.

Internal Links between Pages in a Website

Internal linking, or links among the pages of your website is an important factor for good SEO. You have full control over how and where to place those links, and also include keywords, rather keyword variations, as anchor texts.

It is easy to do, and when done on an ongoing basis, internal linking does help in achieving better search rankings.

To understand the value of internal linking, consider the following situation:

> *Suppose you're stranded inside a big multi-storied mall unable to locate a shop that sells men's shoes. You're contemplating going to the other wing of the mall when suddenly you see a board that gives the details of all the shops in all the floors in the mall, and there you discover that a men's shoe store is indeed close by, just a floor below.*
> *Had this board been not there, you'd have wasted a lot of time, and maybe out of sheer disgust you wouldn't have bought your shoes at all.*

The board in the mall is akin to the concept of internal linking in a website.

In fact the value of internal links should be seen in terms of user experience, and that means the internal links are a great help for the visitors to move around in a website without difficulty.

Here are some excellent examples of internal linking. See some interesting stats below (Figure 4.3), which is that of the book, *The Art of SEO*, in Amazon.Com.

LINKS IN AMAZON.COM PRODUCT PAGE

[http://www.amazon.com/
Art-SEO-Mastering-Optimization-
Practice/dp/0596518862/]

TOTAL LINKS: 456
INTERNAL LINKS: 402
OUTGOING LINKS: 54

Figure 4.3

I get these figures using the Amazon.Com page URL with the *Link Counter Tool*[4.19] of Submit Express to find out the total number of outgoing links on that page.

The page has a total of 456 links of which 402 are internal links and 54 external links. That means over 88% outgoing links are going to Amazon's other pages.

If you do the same test for a product page on eBay, you are likely to get nearly similar results.

This goes to explain the importance of internal links...and this can really help especially when you use keyword variations as anchor texts in the links.

Avoiding the Trap of Duplicate Contents

The phrase, trap of duplicate content, appears too cautionary, but there is a good reason for that. Google dislikes duplicate contents because, quite rightly for them, this can result into poor user experience.

In other words, since Google will always provide the best possible results in response to a search query, it will therefore seek to find the most unique and useful content for that query in its index to be shown in the results.

Duplicate content, by its very nature, puzzles the search engine crawler to decide which one is the actual and original, and makes it difficult to index.

For example, even though there is only one homepage of a website, there could be 4 duplicate pages in the eyes of search engines – *example.com, www.example.com, example.com/index.html,* and *www.example.com/index.html* - each having the same page content.

There are non-intentional (non-malicious in Google's eyes) as well as deceptive and deliberate duplicate contents.

Many people believe that even non-intentional duplicate contents face the wrath of Google with the site being 'banned' or removed from Google's index.

But that is not true. This is what Google says[4.20] on the issue:

Duplicate content on a site is not grounds for action on that site unless it appears that the intent of the duplicate content is to be deceptive and manipulate search engine results. If your site suffers from duplicate content issues, and you don't follow the advice listed above, we do a good job of choosing a version of the content to show in our search results.

However, duplicate content in conjunction with host load limitation (covered in the next section) can be a cause for worry for your website.

To understand how Google tackles the duplicate content issue, do read the relevant Google webmaster guidelines[4.20].

Here are some important points to remember to avoid falling

in the trap of duplicate contents in your website:

1. The header, the sidebars, and the footer are usually the same in all pages of a website. The only thing that separates any 2 pages is the different body content for each page.

2. In cases where the body content changes very little from page to page, the search engines will consider the different pages as having duplicate contents.
An example is that of an online product catalog where the body content has just one product image with a little description.

3. To avoid the problem, it is essential that each page in the site has some content that is unique and the number of words in the content is more than the total number of words in the header, the sidebars, and the footer combined by a safe margin.

4. Ensure that the page title, heading, etc. are different for different pages in your site.

5. Avoid syndicating the same content (an article maybe) you have in your website to any other website. If you are to write in another web publication, substantially change the content before syndicating it.

6. For pages like terms of use for different products, copyright notices, etc. that may have near-similar contents but not important for search rankings, you can include the noindex meta tag in the head section.

7. Use the *rel="canonical"* link element in the head section of a

page to indicate if any URL is a duplicate of another.

In spite of your best efforts, you may still have pages with duplicate contents. It is also possible that other people steal your page content or your syndicated article for unauthorized use in their websites.

In such cases, you may consider using some free online tools to check out the extent of similarity in the contents of 2 pages. Here they are:

- Similar Page Checker[4.21]
- Comparing Duplicate Content[4.22]
- Copyscape Plagiarism Checker – Duplicate Content Detection Software[4.23]
- Plagiarism Checker[4.24]

The Host Load Limitations

The host load limitation is a typical issue in which perhaps you have nothing much to do. It is important however to be aware of this issue.

In an interview[4.25] to Eric Enge, Matt Cutts of Google discusses host load:

> *The host load is essentially the maximum number of simultaneous connections that a particular web server can handle. Imagine you have a web server that can only have one bot at a time. This would only allow you to fetch one page at a time, and there would be a very, very low host load, whereas some sites like Facebook, or Twitter, might have a very high host load because they can take a lot of simultaneous connections.*

Many a small business website resides on shared virtual host server that has a lot of other web sites on the same IP address.

Now if that server has limitations on the number of connections that web crawlers can use to scan all the sites therein, it is obvious that there will be delay in the indexing of the web pages in that server.

Further, as Matt Cutts explains, the delay becomes more if your website happens to have duplicate contents also.

He says:

> *If you happen to be host load limited, and you are in the range where we have a finite number of pages that we can fetch because of your web server, then the fact that you had duplicate content and we discarded those pages meant you missed an opportunity to have other pages with good, unique quality content show up in the index.*

When you study these issues it becomes apparent that you need to be careful about duplicate contents while doing search engine optimization for the pages in your website.

PARTHA BHATTACHARYA

5

WHY CONTENT MATTERS & HOW

I t is easy to understand what web content is. All the stuff you see in a website including texts, images, audio, video, documents, etc. constitute the contents of the site.

Contents are what you now find in a website and all the future stuff as well.

You will agree though that there are web contents you like and there are other web contents that you don't.

For example, why would you like to visit a simple designed website like Wikipedia again and again, and not one that is high on design and colors?

The easy answer is Wikipedia has quality contents that provide value to the visitors, which is something that many other websites don't have.

In other words, design, color, and other eye-catching elements have less or no value to a visitor unless the website has contents that genuinely help him in some way.

Let us dig a bit deeper to understand how and why web content matters both for the visitors and the search engines, and what can be done to improve the contents in a website.

Looks May Betray But Not Content

Take a look at the photos of 2 pastries (Figure 5.1). The one on the left looks thin and ordinary, but the right one looks crisp and freshly baked.

Given a choice, there is little doubt that you'll choose the one on the right.

Yummy, Delicious   Sugary Lump

Figure 5.1

But wait! Suppose somehow you come to know that the left pastry tastes yummy, delicious, and the right pastry has excess of sugar and tastes like a sugary lump.

Which will you now take! No prize guessing the answer!

The difference between a website with good contents and another having a nice flash movie with little else is just like the 2 pastries.

Tell me, do you ever search for information with added conditions like good looking website? For example, would you ever search for the term, *'making money in nice looking website'*?

No one does, and the reason is simple. A visitor wants solid information and not flashy images or something that is good to look at, but tells nothing of value to him.

What Is Web Content?

Let us now look at any webpage. In all likelihood, you'll see texts, images, audio, and video. All of these are web contents, and all of these are communicating something to the visitor.

Now take a look at the HTML code of a typical webpage. Remember search engines robots are machines that are programmed to decipher the HTML codes.

You'll find that all the texts on the webpage appear in full in the HTML code. But – and this is very important – the other contents appear in the code only as file names.

> *Something dot png for the images, something dot mp3 for the audio, something dot mp4 for the video!*

Okay, you know what they are from their file extensions, but from the HTML code do you know how informative and useful they are for the visitor?

You don't!

Which is why for all practical purposes the term web content usually refers to the text contents of a website!

Make no mistake. You need images, audio, and video for enhancing visitor experience and increasing the stickiness of your website.

But none can come at the expense of texts because those are what the search engines understand, and can help in getting better search rankings.

What Is Your Content?

Let's now move on to the more important question, what is your content?

For any business on the web, there are, broadly speaking, 3

factors that play part in shaping the content in your website. They are:

1. Your Knowledge
2. Your Customers' Wants
3. Your Ability to Fulfill Those Wants

Let's briefly discuss each factor and understand the issues that help in deciding the focus of your content.

Your Knowledge

a) When you talk about your knowledge, the first thing to consider is your expertise. Expertise is something that comes by practice from doing something regularly. Often it may be something you're barely aware of.
A good salesman in a shop may be an expert in the art of selling. This is pretty obvious. But he may also be an expert on the buying patterns of consumers, and un-known to him he may possess the rare trait of forecasting the future demands.

b) Having passion is the second important point to consider. In the earlier example, the salesman may be more passionate about selling and less enthusiastic about his unique ability to make demand forecasts.
For him then, the ideal course will be to focus on the art of selling even if apparently there is more money to earn from making forecasts.

c) Going niche is perhaps the most apt concept of successful web content today. To give an example, the art of selling jewelry is not the same as the art of selling real estate. Then again, the art of selling budget houses is not the same as the art of selling villas.

So, ask yourself, "What is my niche?"

Your Customers' Wants

Knowing yourself is the first step for your contents. But this is not very difficult. What is difficult to know is who your customers are and more importantly, what do your customers want?

Fortunately, you have 2 things in your favor. One, because of the Internet the world is your oyster.

No matter what the pundits say, you may be surprised to find that you have customers in a far-flung country beyond your imagination.

The second favorable thing is that people leave their footprints on the web about their wants and wishes.

You only need to mine this vast repertory of data to ferret out the information you need.

There are several ways to go about in this work. An immediate course of action can be to check out some typical places like the Yahoo Answers, Twitter, YouTube, setting Google Alerts, and so on.

Of course, keyword research is a great way to find customers' wants.

Once you have some idea about what your customers' desire is vis-à-vis your knowledge, the next action shifts to evaluating the demand of your knowledge and the supply of it.

If you find the supply is more than the demand, you have to consider a finer niche for your content.

Thus for the real estate salesman in the above example, a further niche to focus could be selling villas on hilltop, or selling villas on causeway, or selling villas near market, and so on.

Your Ability to Fulfill Those Wants

The third factor is equally important as the other two. It is about your ability to fulfill the wants of your customers.

Many well-managed start-ups close down in just 2 or 3 years because they could not meet the pressure of demands.

For web content writing at least 4 issues play a major part for achieving success:

a) Are you ready to write at least 2 articles every week for your website? If you can write more it's better, but in the beginning till your website earns some reputation you need to write pretty often.

b) Are your articles adding value? This one is supreme. Have no doubt in mind about adding value to your posts.

c) Are you prepared to research your topic on the Internet every day? Well, here is the deal. The doors and windows of your mind must be open to all the occurrences of your interests on the web. As you let the ideas flow in, you'll be able to form your own opinion.

d) Are you ready for the long haul? Yes, it is important. Shed the attitude of making quick money. If you wish to make a difference you have to be in there for the long haul.

Crafting Page Title & Headline That Evoke Curiosity

We come to page title again. In the previous chapter we discussed the technical part of page title, and why it is important to have in every webpage. But does the page title by itself provoke the curiosity to read the page content?

Not really! What happens is, unless the page title is irresistible, and the headline equally impressive, the readers will not look into the page content.

In the debate[5.1] – *Can you judge a book by its cover?* – 69% of the respondents say 'Yes', and 31% say 'No'. This may seem bizarre, but that unfortunately is the truth.

Brian Clark of Copyblogger Media sounds a similar caution[5.2] when he says:

> *On average, 8 out of 10 people will read headline copy, but only 2 out of 10 will read the rest. This is the secret to the power of your title, and why it so highly determines the effectiveness of the entire piece.*

And the Intuit Community confirms[5.3] likewise (for an ad in this case):

> *It is a scientifically proven fact that 5 times as many people read headlines as read the body copy of an ad. So with the headline, an advertiser has spent about 80% of their advertising dollar. It doesn't take a genius to realize then the headline is the most important part of any ad.*

So what gives?

Well, since the search engines look for keywords at strategic places including page title and main heading, you have to strike a balance between this necessity and making the duo sufficiently evocative to lure the readers to actually read the page contents.

This can be an onerous task, and is easy said than done.

But you have to do it anyway because it makes no sense if your contents are not read by the readers.

Here is a golden advice. If you use outrageous headlines (not quite literally) readers might lambast you, but they would have read your article at the least.

So what would you prefer? A sedentary title that no one finds exciting to even give a second look, or a spicy headline that provokes some people to read your article!

The choice is yours.

Meanwhile, spend some time and read the following resources:

1. How to Write Magnetic Headlines[5.2]
2. Will You Be E-Mailing This Column? It's Awesome[5.4]
3. Are Your Titles Irresistibly Click-worthy & Viral?[5.5]
4. How To Write Near-Perfect Headlines In Minutes[5.6]

Thinking like Google

There are innumerable articles on the web that advise you how to write contents. Some say, write less but when you write it should be of 'value'.

Others say, write more, and yes, what you write should have 'value' for the readers.

There are advices to write 400-600 words contents, and there are also advices that your posts should be at least 1000 words or more. And again, all that you write should offer 'value' to the readers.

Are you confused? If you are, it is *perfectly* alright.

The point is…all those advices presume that those are what Google thinks.

Is that true?

Well, Google does want the websites to have high quality, useful contents, and its latest algorithms seem to have been programmed to identify the good contents.

I am not a programmer, so I do not know how Google does that. But considering that it really decides what good contents are, does Google specify the exact parameters of good contents?

It doesn't, because it's such a fruitless exercise.

Someone's honey is someone else's poison, so how to decide what is helpful and what is not!

People do not think linearly, so there is no absolute good or absolute bad in the quality of contents on the web.

Instead of wasting time on the effects of Google's thinking, let us look at the logic of that thinking and find out what's best for your business.

And this we will do with the example of a niche shoe store.

Mike wants to set up a shoe store in the main market area. There already is a large shoe store in the market that keeps shoes for both men and women and for both kids and adults. As a result there always is a rush of potential customers in the shop, but he has noticed that a good number among them leave the shop without buying any shoe.

He did a survey among those who don't buy and found that the lack of enough design and variety is the main reason for their not buying anything. He also found that men are more disgruntled than women among the non-buyers.

Mike then set up a niche store selling only men's shoes. This allowed him to keep a large range of shoes in stock, and this helped him quickly garner good many prospective customers who came to visit his shop.

After just 3 months he found that even though the large shoe store gets much more footfalls than his, the percentage conversion from visitor to buyer is much higher in his shop compared to the large store.

Mike did some experiments and found that whenever he changed the shoes kept in the glass showcase just outside the shop, the sales have in-creased. Sales also increased whenever he made some small changes inside the shop in the way the

shoes are displayed.
He figured that making these changes left a positive impact
because people felt his shop had a steady supply of fresh
designs.
Finally, Mike frequently offered special promos like end-of-
week sale, lucky draw, kids contest, etc. and all of these
boosted his sales.

Using the above example as an analogy, we can arrive at the following conclusions for the use of contents in a website:

1. Choosing a niche is more beneficial than pursuing a broad-based website.

2. Writing about problems that people face is always a good idea.

3. Writing frequently leaves a positive impact in the minds of the visitors.

4. Offering some kind of sops now and then is liked by the visitors.

Coming back to thinking like Google, there is perhaps little doubt that the conclusions above are what actually matter when Google asks the webmasters to create contents that offer value to the readers.

The 4 Content Vehicles

By now it should be clear that the contents in a webpage have 2 clients to satisfy – 1) search engines, and 2) users.

However, the funny part is, when they come to a webpage,

the two do not see the same thing.

The search engines, being robots, are programmed to see the HTML code of the page. And in that code the only content that shows up in entirety is the body of texts present in the page.

The other 3 contents – image, audio and video – are seen only as file names (see the section, *What Is Web Content*), and there is no way for the robots to know how good or bad they are.

The users, being humans, see all the contents including image, audio, and video, but they don't see the HTML code (unless they specifically want to).

The humans can therefore analyze and decide the quality of all the contents present in a webpage.

To put in perspective, you need the text contents to satisfy the search engines, and you need the texts plus other contents for your human visitors.

In the next section we will discuss what makes content attractive to read. And after that we will look at the different tools for creating impressive image, audio, and video.

What Makes Your Content Unique

When I started out on my career in my late teens, my mentor had told me:

> *Anything that seeks to create lasting impression is usually the result of detail planning.*

I later found this to be true in all the aspects of our lives.

Think of anything remarkable you come across – the amazing monuments, the extraordinary skills in sports, the quest for outer space, even the epic battles won against adversity – and the odds are that each of them is the culmination of meticulous planning and hard work.

So why should creating contents be any different in your website?

It isn't.

But the problem is to understand what the planning would be for creating contents.

For all it does, web content is the only conduit between a product that is ready for sale and the unseen prospective buyers from any corner of globe who want to buy it.

It therefore has to don the critical role of marketing the product, and also be appealing to a wide section of visitors who want to be informed about product, not necessarily buy it.

To a large extent, uniqueness of content depends on the value it provides to the readers. And mind you, the readers may be anyone from actual buyers to knowledge seekers to even idle gazers.

Given so, what planning can there be to create unique contents?

Take a look at the illustration[5.7] below (Figure 5.2) created by Danyl Bosomworth of *Smart Insights*.

It gives a helpful guideline on how engaging contents can be created with planning.

There are 4 quadrants housing the ideas for creating engaging contents. They are *Entertainment, Educate, Inspire,* and *Convince.*

The content creating ideas correspond to various states of mind, and are good indicators of what to write, and for whom.

To give an example, contents with infographics, trend reports, and guides are useful to educate people.

But you have to move on to more interactive *processes* like case studies, webinars, and interactive demos which are considered as the final steps to convince buyers for making a purchase.

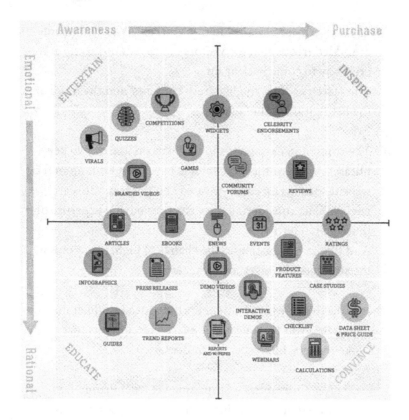

Figure 5.2

There are a few other points to consider for maintaining uniqueness in web contents:

1. The contents in a website will have to be within the niche in which it is operating.

2. Unlike a book that has a beginning and an end, web contents should have a flow of all levels of topics all the time. This is required to cater to the different visitors who have varying interests within your niche.

3. Create fresh contents as often as you can. When new contents are added frequently, the visitors perceive it positively and are likely to come back again.
   The search engines too like fresh contents, and the more of it, the better it is for the website.

4. The content in each page should focus on one or two key-phrases. When sufficient contents have been built up in the website focused on closely related key-phrases, the search engines start considering the website as having expertise on those search terms.
   And that in turn increases the chance of higher rankings in the search result pages for those terms.

5. Irrespective of which content creating idea (as illustrated in Figure 5.2) you're using, some evergreen contents that always evoke readers' interest are as under:

   a. *Negative Stories* – Surprising yet true! People are scared of committing mistakes. So if your story is something like 10 mistakes you want to avoid... you can be assured of visitors' interest.

   b. *How-To Articles* – People like being held by hand for guidance. This is evident when you see articles like How to create a podcast or 5 steps to create your first video are all-time favorites of the readers.

   c. *Statistics & Facts* – There is always an urge to know things beforehand. If you publish an article like 40% web users search for random terms, it is bound to bring interested readers in hordes.

d.   *Lists* – I never stop amazing at the sheer number of list articles like 35 top WordPress plugins, whenever I look for different resources on web design and usability. Greg Habermann, in this Search Engine Watch article[5.8], disclosed that of the 10 most engaging posts of 2012 in SEW, 6 are based around a numeric list.

e.   *Reviews* – Reviews are especially helpful when a new product is launched. Eager buyers invariably rush to read those reviews before making a purchase. Reviews also attract readers when they compare 2 or more products to help in informed decisions.

f.   *Research & Case Studies* – Many readers like in-depth analyses and research before they feel convinced to take an action.
While the end objective is the same (for example, Creating e-learning video in PowerPoint helps), some readers will take your advice at face value, and there will be others who will look for more evidence and reports before taking action.

g.   *Illustrations, Charts, Infographics* – The century-old adage, A picture is worth a thousand words, holds true for attracting readers in any web content. And this is borne out in our everyday experience whether on or off the web.

h.   *Videos, Presentations* – Many enthusiastic writers draw comparison between a video and pictures with that between a picture and words.
While all modes of communication have their own importance, there is no doubt that videos and

presentations are great crowd pullers as can be seen with YouTube and Slideshare.

Refer Jeff Bullas' article[5.9] and Jon Morrow's ebook[5.10] for more on creating unique contents.

Creating Illustrations, Infographics, Other Images

An image on the web is not just a camera picture. It is much more than that.

Charts, graphs, illustrations, clip arts, infographics, screenshots – they all are images in the eyes of search engine robots and each of them has its own rightful importance for attracting and retaining visitor interest in a website.

Many website owners feel more at home writing text articles than creating images, in the fear that it takes more time and is rather a hassle.

In reality when you create an illustrative image like a chart, a graph, or an infographic, you may find it easier to build text contents around the image.

Here are some tools and resources that help you create different types of images for your website:

- *Using PowerPoint* – It's an all-weather tool that helps you create a wide range of images which can then be used in a website.

  a) The *Insert > Screenshot* option allows you to take full or partial screen image. You can then edit it, and also add texts, shapes, or other objects on it. Finally save the whole thing as an image file.

  b) Based on the data you provide, add 11 types of charts

including the difficult ones like doughnut, surface, scatter, bubble, radar, etc. and save as image file.

c)   Create colorful *Smart Arts* that are so useful to explain hierarchical process in a diagram. Similarly, create flow charts using the *Shapes* in PowerPoint.

d)   The *Insert > Clip Art* option allows you to search and embed drawings, illustrations, clip arts, photographs, etc. from Microsoft Office's huge repository.

- *Screenshot Tools* – Several other excellent screenshot tools that are free to use include Gadwin PrintScreen[5.11], Evernote Skitch[5.12], IrfanView[5.13], and others. Each of these tools has lots of features, and you can definitely consider using them for your needs.

- *Free Image Sources* – Nothing beats using an expressive image in a blog post to convey the main thrust of the post. And if you can get it free...nothing like it.
  Among the free image sources that I frequently use are Flickr photos with Creative Commons Attribution License[5.14] and morgueFile free photos[5.15].
  Try out both, especially morgueFile's free photos many of which you can copy, distribute, transmit, and even adapt as you want. Attribution is not required in many cases, but you are prohibited from using the photos in a standalone manner.

- *Button Generators* – Buttons are calls-to-action tools used extensively to entice users to take action in any website. It is easy to create buttons with the help of online tools even if you are not a graphic artiste. 3 free sources to check out are CSS3 Button Generator[5.16], CSS Button Designer[5.17], and CSS

Button Generator[5.18].

- *Infographic Tools* – If you are a frequent user of PowerPoint you may feel at home creating infographics with the various tools available there. There however are some excellent free online tools to create just the infographic you want.

1. *Google Charts*[5.19] –
   Google provides a variety of charts that are optimized for different data optimization needs. Once you create the right one for your requirement, you can embed the chart in any webpage.

2. *easel.ly*[5.20] –
   With easel.ly you can create visual idea by dragging and dropping visual themes or vhemes onto your canvas.

3. *Creately*[5.21] –
   Creately is the tool to create flow charts, mind maps, UML, wire frames, etc. and an extensive library is provided to you for that. It has the real-time collaboration feature that allows you to work with a colleague or client simultaneously.

4. *Visual.ly*[5.22] –
   Visual.ly offers the option of using templates that help you create infographics based around Twitter or Facebook data.

5. *Piktochart*[5.23] –
   Piktochart gives the option of using 6 free templates (more when you upgrade) which you can use to create

your own infographic. You may create charts manually, or by uploading chart data in a CSV file.

6.   *infogr.am*[5.24] –
     Yet another tool to create infographic is infogr.am. Like others, this tool also gives 6 templates, and is very easy to use. It is also an ideal tool for creating standalone charts.

Creating Audio Podcast

Perhaps one of the least used media content is web audio in any website. This may be because the extensive use of video has overshadowed the utility of audio as a content marketing tool in a website.

Fortunately, voice recording, editing, merging with music, and producing the final MP3 audio is quite easy, and this can be done with free tools like Audacity[5.25].

What's more, you can source free, royalty-free music[5.26] which you can then use with your voice recording as a background tune.

Finally, there are free tools available on the web to embed an audio file in any webpage. If you use WordPress, consider the plugins WP Audio Player[5.27] or oEmbed HTML5 audio[5.28] for inserting audio in any page or post.

Creating Web Video

In an earlier chapter we have discussed how YouTube has emerged as the second most popular search engine on the web after Google edging out Bing and Yahoo.

And this has become possible because of huge surge in people's interest to watch videos.

That being so, it can be said without an iota of doubt that video is today an essential content building tool for any website.

However, creating a video still looks like a difficult job for many webmasters. This shouldn't be!

In my long experience as a video maker I have seen that many people do not realize that they can easily make a large variety of video from PowerPoint.

They consider PowerPoint as a tool for making presentation, and get surprised when shown that it is easy to make video with it.

In fact there is no tool quite like PowerPoint that makes it super easy to create videos with animated graphs, charts, smart arts, clip arts, shapes, texts, and images. Why, even video-on-video can be made effortlessly with PowerPoint.

With so much to do with PowerPoint it'll indeed be tough not to get inspired to create video that can be uploaded to YouTube, and embedded in any webpage.

To make the job easy for amateur video makers, I have made an extensive course titled, *How to Make Sleek Professional Video with PowerPoint*[5.29].

If you are interested to learn the course, contact me at team@hubskills.com for up to *90% discount* in the price of the course.

6
ADVANCED SEO CONSIDERATIONS

The purpose of SEO shall not remain confined within the narrow alleys of keyword research and on-page techniques only. The need to reach out is real and cannot be overlooked at any cost.

Many experts suggest that search engines follow traffic. If a website or a webpage is being visited by a large number of people coming from different sources other than search results, then the search engines will sit up and take notice of that very quickly.

In other words, spare no effort to break out from the mold of copybook style of SEO, and do everything ethically possible to spread the influence of your website.

In this chapter we will discuss some of the steps that enhance the ability of a website to be seen by more visitors.

The emphasis is on envisioning the bigger picture that can rapidly grow your website while helping it mature over time.

Image Optimization

A significant part of the information available on the net consists of images. Starting from logos and headings to charts, graphs, and myriad pictorial illustrations, there is no dearth of images that, like texts, support the information being conveyed to the surfers who scour the net.

Though images are long-standing companions for texts, people barely search for them exclusively for informational needs. They rather look for images which in some instances they can replicate or suitably alter for their requirement.

From search engines' point of view, there is no way telling how good and relevant an image is at the place of its usage except for 3 parameters:

1.   Name of the image,
2.   Title of the image, and
3.   Alt attribute of the image

As can be seen, it is easy to manipulate all the 3 parameters to give the search engines a false idea of keyword relevance even while showing a completely irrelevant image.

This is a dangerous game to play for the sake of 'SEO on the fast lane' simply because such tricks inevitably bring down the goodwill and the prestige of a website.

As opposed to text optimization for the search engines, there is generally an absence of clear-cut directives for optimizing images.

This may be partly because of the accepted views that the search engines cannot yet decipher the actual content of rich media like images, and whatever is available for consideration is nothing but texts associated with them.

However, based on user experience, some important factors with regard to image optimization are explained below:

1. Use descriptive name for the image file that has the keyword phrase in it.
    For example, if a page is on fashion jewelry, then you can name the jewelry image in the page something like 'glittering-set-of-fashion-jewelry.jpg'.

2. The image title is said to have no SEO-related importance. Yet in many browsers, the visitors see it while moving the cursor on the image.

   For that reason it is better not to omit the image title. This too can be made lengthier while using a variation of keyword phrase. For example, it can be 'Designer jewelry for fashion is a must wear'.

3. Alt attribute is considered the most important from SEO point of view. Here is what Jill Whalen, the SEO expert, has to say[6.1]:

   But the alt attribute text of clickable images seems to be treated very similarly to anchor text in an all-text link.

   Note there are 2 issues here. One, the image has to be clickable, and two, the alt attribute text is similar to anchor text in an all-text link.

   The alt attribute should have the keyword phrase, but once again, use it in a long sentence.

   Example of embedding a clickable image with the title and alt attribute is as under:

   <a href=""><img src="glittering-set-of-fashion-jewelry.jpg" title=" Designer jewelry for fashion is a must wear" alt="Affordable designer fashion jewelry" width="" height=""/></a>

4. It is better to be cautious and not use the keyword phrase in the alt attributes of more than 2 images in a single webpage. Else, it may be considered as spam by search engines.

5. According to some experts[6.2] the text near the image in the

HTML is also important, and also the image age.

6. An image is considered authoritative based on the page it links to upon clicking, and what other pages, if any, link to it.

7. In eye-tracking experiments[6.3] jointly by The Poynter Institute and 2 others, it has been found that larger online images hold the eye longer than smaller images.
    At least 210 x 230 pixels in size were viewed by more than half of the testers, and clean, clear faces in images attract more eye fixations on homepages.

Researchers routinely conduct various studies to understand how online images are perceived by the visitors, and what, if any, can be done to the images to ensure enriching user experience in a webpage.

Authority of Your Website – Relevant Contents

People love authority. They like command. These are the qualities that give them the satisfaction of being at the right place at the right time.

Search engines follow (rather, made to follow through logic-supported algorithms) these human traits rather closely. And why not!

Picture yourself looking for information on royal Bengal tiger for one of your projects. When you search for the term you'll come across results that show quite a few pages from the tourism sites.

But the ones that rank at the top are from the prestigious content sites like Wikipedia, National Geographic, and the like. You are likely to visit these pages since your need is to collect reliable information for your project.

The search engines give importance to the pages from the websites that command authority on the strength of the contents they contain. This 'strength' is not built overnight. It accrues to a website over a length of time when the site goes on adding pages of relevant contents optimized for search engines.

I have extensively dealt on web contents in the earlier chapters. But to summarize again, here are 4 important factors to consider:

1. Build contents for your website having relevance with the main thrust of the site. For example, in a website on web video production, continually have contents that concern with the different aspects of video making.

2. Each content page needs to be optimized for one or two relevant key-phrases. This will work as a signal to the search engine robots as to the importance of that webpage with respect to the chosen key-phrase.

3. Keep on accumulating relevant contents.

4. Ensure that the contents you create, though relevant, are actually helpful to your readers, and not some gibberish only aimed for ranking.

Authority of Your Website – Incoming Links

Perhaps the most sought-after and prized gifts for any website are incoming hyperlinks to it from other websites. This is one asset the need of which never ceases, both for the website concerned and other websites that link to it.

Incoming links are obvious stamps of authority. The famous

link analysis algorithm, PageRank, named after Google founder Larry Page, is an indicator of the importance of a webpage as viewed by Google.

Google describes PageRank[6.4] as under:

PageRank reflects our view of the importance of web pages by considering more than 500 million variables and 2 billion terms. Pages that we believe are important pages receive a higher PageRank and are more likely to appear at the top of the search results.

PageRank also considers the importance of each page that casts a vote, as votes from some pages are considered to have greater value, thus giving the linked page greater value. We have always taken a pragmatic approach to help improve search quality and create useful products, and our technology uses the collective intelligence of the web to determine a page's importance.

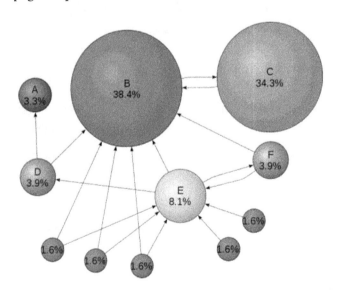

Figure 6.1

From the pictorial illustration[6.5] of PageRank above (Figure 6.1) above it is clear that getting incoming links from good quality webpages should be a priority for any website owner.

The reality is however quite harsh.

No one gives links on request unless the link-donor decides that doing so will fetch rewards. This aspect needs to be understood clearly.

Large authoritative sites whose links do count a lot will hardly bother to give links to a startup.

Those that give when approached may perhaps ask for favors in return that may prove costly for startups.

Small and medium websites often spend good amount of resources to get incoming links from others, which in case of authority websites is akin to chasing the mirage.

In the long run, such do-or-die efforts spread the resources so thin that the website itself becomes unviable to run properly.

The best advice therefore will be to first build authority of your website with relevant contents, and only after that there can be moderate attempts toward the goal of getting quality incoming links.

Apart from creating quality contents over a period of time, there can be a 2-pronged approach to build authority of your website through links by:

1. Giving stress on internal linking among the pages of your website with keyword variations as anchor texts. This must be followed to the maximum extent, especially since this is well within the control of the website owner.

2. Reaching out to get links, like writing in top web publications, guest-blogging, and so on (covered in the next chapter).

Speed Of Website Pages

Why and how is website speed important? Let us hear from horse's mouth. This is what Google has to say in the Official Google Webmaster Central Blog[6.6]:

> *You may have heard that here at Google we're obsessed with speed, in our products and on the web. As part of that effort, today we're including a new signal in our search ranking algorithms: site speed. Site speed reflects how quickly a website responds to web requests.*

2 things become clear from the above.

1. Google is obsessed with site speed, and so
2. Site speed is an important parameter in Google's search ranking algorithms.

This means how fast or slow your webpage loads in a browser is one determining factor (among others) in the rankings of Google's search results.

Google's internal studies[6.7] have shown that slowing down the search results page by 100 to 400 milliseconds has a measurable impact on the number of searches per user, which, though seemingly small, has real consequence at the scale of Google web search.

Google goes on to say that it encourages site designers to think twice about adding a feature that hurts performance if the benefit of the feature is unproven.

There is pretty much you, as a website owner, can do to improve the speed of your website. Yahoo Developer Network (YDN) has charted out best practices for speeding up web site[6.8]. Some among them are as under:

1. Minimize HTTP requests
2. Use a Content Delivery Network
3. Put style sheets at the top
4. Put scripts at the bottom
5. Make JavaScript and CSS external
6. Minify JavaScript and CSS
7. Avoid redirects
8. Remove duplicate scripts
9. Minimize the number of iframes
10. Optimize images

How to Know Page Speed

To be cautioned is a good idea, but even better is to be able to have a good measurable data of that. There are quite a few tools that Google and Yahoo suggest using to find out the loading time of the webpages.

A few of them are mentioned below:

1. *Yahoo YSlow*[6.9] analyzes web pages and suggests ways to improve their performance based on a set of rules for high performance web pages. It is a Firefox add-on[6.10], and has the Firebug web development tool integrated with it.

2   Similar to YSlow, *Page Speed*[6.11] is the tool for optimizing the performance of webpages. This also is a Firefox/Firebug add-on, and has later been utilized in some third-party products.

3. *WebPagetest*[6.12] is based on the technology of Page Test, but it's an online tool. You have to enter a website URL, and start testing. A little later you'll get the page's performance in both analytical and visual formats.

4. *Pingdom Tools*[6.13] is my favorite. Like WebPagetest, this one too is available online (see Figure 6.2). It is fast and provides good amount of information like total loading time, total objects, number of scripts and images, and so on.
   The results also give a glimpse of the size and the time taken by each object to load in the page.

Figure 6.2

Age of Website

There is a lot of conjecture about the age of a website playing a prominent role in Google's algorithms for search ranking. Many people feel older websites are seen favorably by Google, while others say that more than the website, it's the age of the domain name that is more important.

The truth is not known because Google, to the best of my knowledge, has not commented upon the matter.

You may like to think that if at all Google gives preference to older sites then all the new web ventures, howsoever attractive, will always remain at a disadvantage.

This looks unlikely. If however a new website with a new

domain gets prominence with lots of incoming links in a short time, then it can raise doubts in Google's minds.

This is something that some years back was referred to as the Sandbox effect[6.14].

Having said that, when you are going to start a new website consider the following domain-related steps as enumerated by webconfs.com[6.15].

1. Make sure you register your domain name for the longest amount of time possible.

2. Consider registering a domain name even before you are sure you're going to need it.

3. Think about purchasing a domain name that was already pre-owned.

4. Keep track of your domain's age. One of the ways you can determine the age of a domain is with this handy Domain Age Tool[6.16].

7

GETTING LINKS BY REACHING OUT

There are many factors to consider when you make plans to get links from other websites. This is a tricky job, and we will soon see why.

In the early days of SEO, one way to rank high in search results was to get incoming links from other websites – any website for that matter.

This resulted in mushrooming of link farms of different shades whose only job was to get you links, often at a big price.

This defeated the very purpose of Google considering links as votes of approval, because if you can buy links, the quality of contents is bound to take the backseat.

To counter this epidemic of artificially inflating the chances of higher rankings, Google brought in drastic changes in its algorithm since the beginning of 2011.

The main changes are codenamed Panda and Penguin, and have different updates belonging to them including the penalization for link farming and content scraping.

In recent times you may have come across Google's advice[7.1] that says:

> *In general, webmasters can improve the rank of their sites by creating high-quality sites that users will want to use and share.*

It may surprise you, but not long back Google's advice was to increase the number of high quality sites that link to their pages.

Look at the image (Figure 7.1) showing Google's change of stance between October 2012 and May 2013. It was first noticed by Erik Baemlisberger[7.2].

Ranking

Sites' positions in our search results are determined based on a number of factors designed to provide end-users with helpful, accurate search results. These factors are explained in more detail at http://www.google.com/competition/howgooglesearchworks.html

In general, webmasters can improve the rank of their sites by increasing the number of high-quality sites that link to their pages. For more information about improving your site's visibility in the Google search results, we recommend reviewing our Webmaster Guidelines. They outline core concepts for maintaining a Google-friendly website.

updated 10/16/2012

Ranking

Sites' positions in our search results are determined based on hundreds of factors designed to provide end-users with helpful, accurate search results. These factors are explained in more detail at http://www.google.com/competition/howgooglesearchworks.html

In general, webmasters can improve the rank of their sites by creating high-quality sites that users will want to use and share. For more information about improving your site's visibility in the Google search results, we recommend visiting Webmaster Academy which outlines core concepts for maintaining a Google-friendly website.

updated 05/27/2013

Figure 7.1

Looking at this clear indication from Google, it would appear that any kind of 'conscious link-building' is passé. I've discussed in this chapter several supposedly out-of-favor link-building concepts like press release, submitting to article directories, etc. and I've done that to emphasize the logic of reaching out to prospects where they are hanging out, rather than seeking only links.

At the end of the day it is the readers who will like to use their discretion to pursue link-building avenues as deemed fit for their purpose.

Have Links Lost Luster?

Due to the changes in Google's algorithm, getting high-quality links has become well-nigh impossible. In How to Fix the Broken Link Graph[7.3], Aaron Wall makes some interesting observations:

- No one links honestly any more.
- All links are suspect.
- No one links freely any more.

This may sound a bit pessimistic but there are good reasons for that. Because of Google's updates, which many experts feel was anyway due for a long time, people are wary to ask for or give links.

Does that mean there is no value in incoming links? Not really!

In a July 2013 interview[7.4] to Eric Enge, Google's Matt Cutts says:

> *Link building is not illegal. Not all link building is bad. The philosophy that we've always had is if you make something that's compelling then it would be much easier to get people to write about it and to link to it.*

It is clear then that the path to build links is to create great contents…to which the links would come naturally, automatically.

When you do this, you don't go seeking links. They come without your making any special effort.

This finds resonance with the concept, "build it, and they'll come". A good example of that is reflected in this interview[7.5] with Fraser Cain, owner of Universe Today. Fraser says:

Focus 100 percent of your effort on your own website and the needs of your audience. Even brand new websites will bring in long tail search traffic from the search engines if they solve problems for people. The problem is that people immediately try to focus on rankings; and that's where the massive link building campaigns come in. But if you focus only on increasing your overall search traffic, and not battle for any specific keyword, your traffic just grows and grows.

The traffic to Fraser's website has increased from 3500 visits a day to a phenomenal 100,000+ unique visitors every day by (1) building contents, and (2) not doing any *conscious* link building campaign.

Options for Small Website

Though Fraser Cain's example is highly motivating, for many small websites things may be tough in actual practice. Fraser's niche is astronomy, and it does seem that a lot can be written in that subject.

No one denies that writing lots of targeted relevant content is good for a website, but for many small websites, too much emphasis on contents may compromise with running the business.

For them large traffic from search results is often a dream than reality.

In this backdrop, link-getting exercise for small websites should be seen in the context of reaching out to the prospects.

The need for reaching out arises since the prospects have different places to hang out on the web. In each of those places they are looking for the product or service your website is offering.

What are those places, and how you can reach there?

In this chapter we will look at some of those places. The basic surmise is that search engine optimization, though crucially important, is not a magic bullet. It is not something you do to the exclusions of all other promotional campaigns.

The options we will examine here range from simple article writing in other websites to embracing social media, and more.

It may be the case that you cannot manage sufficient resources for all of these. After all you have your business and your website to look after.

Those dilemmas are solvable by involving/outsourcing some works to other people or agencies (covered in more detail in Chapter 8).

And if that is something you are not comfortable with or have other bottlenecks, it is better to start with minimum efforts for reaching out.

Whatever it is that you plan, there's one thing you shouldn't lose sight of. It's about doing *something* at least, because as I said above, a whole bunch of opportunities awaits you outside the ambit of SEO.

Avail them.

Write In Web Publications

If you extend the logic to the web as a whole that content is the mainstay of any website, it becomes clear that there ought to be giant, content-heavy sites that can be the destinations for your needs.

2 such web publications are Hubpages[7.6] and Squidoo[7.7]. Both are free to enroll, and have their own loyal base of users, though (without taking sides) more users seem to be happy using Hubpages.

Here briefly are some of the common features that both Hubpages and Squidoo offer:

1. Write texts, include images, and even embed videos from video sharing sites in your article, called a hub in Hubpages and a lens in Squidoo.

2. Earn money from your articles through your affiliate ads from Google AdSense, Amazon, Ebay, and others.

3. Get ratings for the articles that you write from the users. Higher rating means more exposure and more traffic.

4. Embed links in your articles that point to the pages in your website. If the rating of an article is good there is just a chance (at least with Hubpages) that the embedded links will not be 'nofollowed'[7.8].

5. Viewers can comment in your articles, giving you chance to engage with them. Similarly, when you comment in others' articles you enhance your standing as being a good user.

6. You are discouraged to write duplicate contents by Hubpages. Before you can submit your article in Hubpages for example, it is checked real-time for duplicity, and cleared only when it is found to be not so.

Most of these features are not available in article directories, which is why writing in a web publication like Hubpages is a good proposition.

Guest Blogging

Let me start from the site of Mashable[7.9], a hugely popular news site for social and digital media that actively seeks a story from anyone. Mashable has an Alexa ranking of 458, and Compete ranking of 1224 as of this writing.

Mashable is not alone. Many top technology blogging sites, like ClickZ[7.10], SitePoint[7.11], BloggingPro[7.12], Smashing Magazine[7.13], and others invite guest writers to post in their sites.

The reason is not far to seek.

Blog sites need articles posted daily, and at the same time it is far beneficial for them to get free writings of good quality from talented guest writers from all over the globe. The latter get exposure and backlinks in return and occasionally maybe some money as compensation.

There is no dearth of information to be gleaned about guest blogging on the web. Jonathan Morrow of Copyblogger, for example, offers a membership course[7.14] to learn 'everything' about guest blogging.

And Ann Smarty, herself an accomplished guest blogger, has not long back started My Blog Guest[7.15], a meeting ground for both guest bloggers and those looking for guest posts.

There is a subtle difference between guest blogging and writing in web publications (covered in the previous section) on one hand, and between it and submission to article directories (covered next) on the other.

Let me mention some points below for you to mull over:

1 Web publications like Hubpages are not focused on particular topic(s). There you find tips on parenting babies, and also on making money from Google AdSense. A blog inviting guest writing is usually focused on a niche topic and rarely publishes articles on other topics. An article directory is similar to a web publication in this respect.

2 As against hundreds of posts being published in article directories and web publications every day, a blog will usually have 2-3 (or less) highly focused posts each day. Since a blog-

post is more relevant and targeted toward the right section of readers, it therefore receives the right kind of exposure.

3   Guest articles are subject to scrutiny by the blog owner. An article may be edited, and if not liked, may not be published in the blog. Often a guest post may not be allowed images or videos to come along with it. You don't find these restrictions in web publications, though article directories too don't accept images or videos in many cases.

4   A backlink from a guest-post supposedly carries more weight than the other two simply because the blog is more focused on a relevant topic.

5   Guest-posts may not receive any remuneration from the blogs though a few exceptions are there. Article directories too make you no money. Some web publications like Hubpages do however share earnings from the ads in the article pages.

Would You Use Article Directories?

At the outset let me caution that links from the article directories no longer help. In fact, many experts suggest[7.16] *stopping adding article directory links right away. And in case you still have some, then work on getting them removed.*

This is one of the easiest ways to ramp up inbound links around anchor texts to the deeper pages of your website. Since it's you who 'cultivates' these links, therefore the entry barrier to derive benefits from article directories is quite low.

And so there is always the usual rush to submit articles to these sites as soon as a website is up and running.

People look at article directories purely with a view to

embedding links, which is perhaps one reason why good quality contents are just not available there. Given these factors, it is fully your discretion whether to strategize for article marketing as a means to build links.

In case you are inclined to try out article marketing, you might want to study some best practices and guidelines for article submission as suggested by Ken Lyons of WordStream[7.17].

A few tips are as under:

- Don't add links in the body of the article. Links to your site should reside in the bio or "about the author" section.

- Keep links in the bio to a maximum of 3. More than three can/will get your article rejected.

- Don't promote your company in the body of the article. Save that for the bio section.

- Do not plagiarize. It doesn't help. Your article will not be published in the better ones. You can however "repackage" your own content.

- Don't stuff your articles with keywords. Many submission sites have stringent rules to test "keyword density" in articles submitted.

- Ensure there are no misspellings or grammatical errors.

Leave Comments in Blogs

When starting out for the first time, it almost feels like a 'nobody' in the vast wonderland of the web. You want to get counted but no one really cares. You add contents in your website, and you do the entire copybook SEO you've learnt. Yet you are still stranded on the sidelines.

In situations like this which we all face one time or the other, the trick to get 'known' quickly and easily is to leave comments in other blogs.

In most blogs you can leave your URL in the comment box to act as incoming link, but usually it is marked as 'nofollow'[7.8].

That means you don't get the advantage of the incoming link for ranking purpose. However, let that not stop you from commenting in the blogs, for otherwise you will miss out on some great intangible benefits.

Darren Rowse, founder of Problogger, strongly recommends[7.18] the practice of leaving comments in the other blogs. Some advantages are as under:

- Get to know what other bloggers in your niche are doing.

- This is a great chance to build your own profile in your niche, and show your expertise, knowledge and understanding of the topic.

- If your comment triggers remarks by others, you have a chance to know what others have to say on the topic (this may help you write more articles on the topic).

- You'll be able to reach out to other bloggers who get the chance to gauge your understanding of the topic involved (often comments begin the start of fruitful relationships).

- Your thoughtful comments in another blog are in fact a small window for the readers of that blog to come and visit your website.
  The downside of leaving comment in another blog is often

negligible, but you need to be cautious anyway. Here are some points that you need to pay attention to.

- Since you're a guest in another blog, you should not be harsh in your comment, or use bad words. Needless to say, they are never published by the blog owner.

- If your comment is criticized, and you feel that is not correct, do make a counter reply. Rebut firmly, but avoid using hard words. In fact you have a good chance to speak out your mind, which you shouldn't spoil by being curt.

- Don't talk big or write something that is untrue. People have ways to quickly find out the truth.

- Don't write frivolous or out-of-context comments. They will never be published. If you nothing worthy to say, say nothing.

- Aiming for only backlink in the comments is a bad idea. People often use a key-phrase in the name field for backlink. Such an effort never succeeds.

Participate In Forums

An Internet forum is defined[7.19] as a kind of message board where online discussions take place involving participants who hold conversations in the form of posted messages.

The key to the success of a forum lies in the willingness of the participants to actively put forth their points of view to seek replies from the other members. In doing so, the forum members reach out to help or seek help from others.

There is usually no restriction to become a forum member,

though there are many instances of private forums that allow only paying members to participate in the forum discussions.

The advantage of actively participating in the forums of your niche is that you can subtly enhance your profile and your value as a person of knowledge over time among the other members.

This can help you in getting substantial traffic originating from the forum. This traffic is quite worthy since the people are coming after having known about your ability in the forum.

To quote[7.20] Darren Rowse (of Problogger) again, he explains (via an anonymous blogger) an 8-step approach to gather traffic by participating in the forums. They are very practical and indeed achievable.

Here they are in brief:

1. Identify the forums where your blog's potential readers are gathering. It may not suit you to become members of many forums at a time.
   Instead, start with a prominent forum in your niche that gets good traffic and has many members. Gradually you may increase participation in more of them over time.

2. Join up, and do nothing. This according to the writer is a key step. Lurk around and learn who the key players are, what topics are the hottest, and which areas of the forum are the most active. This learning will prove helpful in the coming days.

3. Set up your signature and an avatar or your image. Let the signature be brief, and not flashy or boastful. That doesn't help.

4. Start posting. Initially, it is better to make yourself helpful to the other members. Answer the problems faced by them. At

least till a few weeks have passed by, the time is not ripe to promote own blog or posts.

5. Write resourceful contents in forum posts. These can be short tutorials having useful information which you would have otherwise posted in your blog. Gradually, people start taking notice of your knowledge, and get drawn to you.

6. Make connections. Reaching out to other active and influential members of the forum will be the next step. Send private messages to them with words of encouragement. They will really appreciate the gesture from your side, and it will be easy for you to keep them in the loop for any future need of yours.

7. Let others promote your blog. A few weeks after you prove your worth, a lot of forum members may voluntarily promote you and your blog to others. This may seem surprising, but this is true.

8. Be generous, understated, and useful. This according to me is the most useful tip. The more subtle you are, the more success you reap.

Send Press Releases

There is a hot debate about the desirability of press releases by small businesses. Many people feel that paying for press release is a waste of money because the benefit may not match the cost involved.

That may be partly true, especially with regard to the benefits accruing from incoming link. However when your website is new and no one knows about it, you have to do something to spread the word. Press release fits the bill perfectly.

There are big agencies like PRWeb[7.21], or personalized services like that by Eric Ward's URLwire[7.22] that may cost a lot of money.

They may produce good results, but perhaps it is wiser for a small business to not pay the high amounts for press release.

Instead they may try out the free services of Free Press Release[7.23], PRLog[7.24], and others. There is no harm in trying out the free services except that the typical press release format is strictly adhered to.

Otherwise, many a time, press releases are not accepted.

Some good read-outs for knowing more about press releases, including the usual Dos and Don'ts are given below:

- Press Release Writing Tips From the New York Times[7.25]
- 5 Killer Press Release Tips for Small Businesses[7.26]
- Stand Out: The Power Of The Press Release[7.27]

Create Video & Upload to YouTube

This may be a little radical of all the different ways described here, but it is worth doing. The good thing about video is that it is easy to do.

But what, you may wonder, is the need to make videos? The answer is rather simple. Going by the huge and increasing popularity the video is enjoying on the web it makes good sense to ride the wave and reach out to a large audience.

The following chart (Figure 7.2) shows how the number of video viewers is increasing in the US over the years. It is the same in almost all the web-savvy countries in the world.

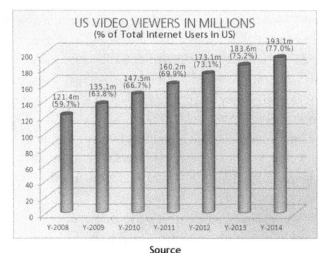

Figure 7.2

Many small business owners however are not comfortable with the idea of web video. They feel it is difficult to make, and of course it is beyond their means to hire a professional who may charge a lot to make one.

The truth is it costs almost none to make a web video from scratch as explained in the section *Creating Web Video* (Chapter 5).

You can quite easily make sleek, professional web video with PowerPoint for many of your needs like training video, marketing video, e-learning video, illustrative video, and so on.

Watch the different PowerPoint videos in action in my PowerPoint to video course at Udemy[7.28]. If interested, contact me at team@hubskills.com for up to *90% rebate* on my course.

Remember web video is not only about movie shot with a video camera. It can be made from screen-recording, flash movie, PowerPoint, and also static images.

Once you try out doing any one kind of video, your

confidence will increase and shortly you may start making other types of videos.

When you upload your video to YouTube, just grab the embed code from there and put it in your website. Thus, your own video is displayed on your site though it is hosted on YouTube.

The importance of video marketing for your business becomes clear because of dramatic increase in the number of video-hours uploaded to YouTube per minute in a short span of 3 years.

In other words, you cannot afford to ignore video marketing at the cost of letting your competition go past you.

Create Your Facebook Page

The rise of Facebook can be attributed to the massive awakening of people's desire to know what others are doing, and to let know what they are doing.

In the database of intentions as of early 2010[7.29], famous blogger John Battelle has lucidly explained the dramatic evolving of search behavior on the web and the role being played by major players including Facebook.

John explains that today the people's intention on the web is not only to query search engines, but also to express themselves through social graphs and status updates.

In other words, the popularity of online social media outlets like Facebook, Twitter and others will continue to rise, and may in fact accelerate further.

As if to bolster John's contention, comScore first reported Facebook having surpassed Google in August 2010 in the US in terms of time spent in their sites[7.30].

The trend continues…and recently it was found[7.31] that in the US Facebook enjoys more time spent on the site (10.8%) than

Google (10%). What's more, of all time spent on social networking sites, 83% is spent on Facebook.

The same is reflected in the chart below (Figure 7.3) taken from Hitwise[7.32] that puts Facebook as the most popular social media website.

Top 10 Social Media Websites

Week ending July 20, 2013

Websites	Total Visits	Visits Share ▼	Rank 07/13	Rank 07/06	Rank 06/29
Facebook	1,964,045,691	56.20%	1	1	1
YouTube	873,819,912	25.00%	2	2	2
Twitter	67,359,854	1.93%	3	3	3
Linkedin	42,096,410	1.20%	4	5	4
Pinterest	35,826,013	1.03%	5	4	5
Yahoo! Answers	32,774,450	0.94%	6	6	6
Google+	31,525,245	0.90%	7	7	7
Instagram	17,279,819	0.49%	8	10	10
Tumblr	16,974,092	0.49%	10	8	8
Tagged	16,583,775	0.47%	9	9	9

Figure 7.3

There are skeptics though who feel[7.33] that the overtaking of Google by Facebook is perhaps a non-event, because when it comes to translating "viewers" into revenue, Google currently wins hands down.

However, there is no denying the huge euphoria around the social media sites, particularly Facebook and Twitter. And so it is a good idea for a small business to embrace both with open arms.

There are many free advisories that give instructions on how to create your Facebook page and reap benefits from its large array of features. Let me point you to the excellent article, Facebook Marketing: Ultimate Guide[7.34], published in Moz.

Some useful tips given by the author are as under:

- "Page Name" is one of the strongest ranking factors on Facebook search. Take the opportunity to add some keywords you wish to rank for in your page name. Remember you are not allowed to change your page name later.

- When you type a URL starting from http:// in the info box under your profile picture, Facebook makes it into a clickable link. Don't forget to include URLs here that lead to the webpages you want.

- Once you have at least 25 fans, you will be able to convert your ugly "326727833086?ref=sgm&ajaxpipe=1&__a=7" URL into something fancy-looking, like "http://facebook.com/mybusinesspage".

- Make your landing page attractive. Great first looks will convert more of your visitors into fans.

- When you compose a message, make a habit of putting the '@' symbol and start typing the name of your business page to mention it, just the way you mention someone on Twitter or in blog replies.

- Facebookers usually prefer pictures, videos and links to plain text updates. So use these resources liberally.

- You must aim to build partnerships with other Facebookers within your niche and be "favourited" as much as possible.

- Write an engaging request to join your Facebook page and set it in your Twitter account as an automatic direct message to people, who have just followed you.

- Make videos, and when you host them in a video sharing site, use annotations to include a link to your Facebook page with a request to join.

- Put the link to your Facebook page everywhere – on your website, your business card, in every opportunity you get.

Start Tweeting

Twitter was launched in July 2006, and initially few people thought it would ever attain the rage it has now.

As explained in the previous section, quoting John Battelle's analysis of people's intentions online, the desire to know others and tell about oneself have fueled the phenomenal growth of Twitter and other social media vehicles.

Twitter allows text-based posts of up to 140 characters by the members. The posts are called tweets and can be about anything you want to share with others.

Becoming a member is free, and so is the sending of posts. No wonder, many term tweets as the SMSs of the Internet though the latter are not actually free.

Currently, as of this writing, Twitter is estimated[7.35] to have over 550 million users all over the world, who generate an average of 58 million tweets a day (9100 tweets every second), and do 2.1 billion searches a day. That's massive, which is why using this free social media platform is very important.

There are many how-to articles about using and benefitting from Twitter. Opening an account and starting to use it are really easy. So the best advice will be to start tweeting right away, and find yourself what works, and what doesn't.

As with other social media tools, with Twitter too you need to follow a strategy to reap the harvest of benefits. You may like to read the PCMag.com article[7.36], *How to Use Twitter for Business.*

Compared to Facebook, tweeting is easy. The best part is you start getting instant attention every time you tweet.

So, each time you write an article or upload a video or find something interesting, you can share with the world by tweeting about it.

If liked by others, they may retweet your post, spreading your word fast.

Participate In Seminars, Symposiums, Workshops

Notice all of those I've mentioned above so far involve online efforts, or those that are done on the web.

Surely you expect that your prospects could come from the offline – or, let me call this the brick-n-mortar world – sources as well. So you need to reach out to these targets also.

Usually the common approach to target the offline prospects is to place ads in the local newspapers. This is a proven concept, and maybe you should opt for packages for several insertions spanning over a few months.

Many marketers however feel that since newspapers have time-limited relevance, therefore the ads are overlooked easily despite the reach to a seemingly large number of readers.

Moreover, in an age of laser-focused online advertising as in Facebook for example, newspaper ads can be said to be lacking the muscle of targeted reach.

What better ways could there be for your products to reach those who matter? Talk-shows like the seminars, symposiums, and workshops are the answers for that.

How you proceed in such cases depends much on the twin aspects of the size of your company and the size of the likely populace to target.

If you haven't done one already, you may perhaps think of holding a free or a paid (why not?) seminar where you arrange an industry expert to give the keynote address.

This effort can prove to be quite costly (which is why the question of how big your company is!). On the flip side you'll be able to target the right prospects, and also take the opportunity to survey the participants to get a first-hand idea about your product.

Alternatively, take part in such gatherings as a participant and try to reach out to the other participants. If conditions permit, you may think of advertising your product in the seminar area by putting up banners or distributing leaflets to the visitors who come there to attend.

The underlying mantra to reap benefits in such cases is always to be at the right place at the right time.

Local Reputation Matters

Have you wondered who your best friends are during adversity? Give it a thought and chances are that the local community is the one you can think of as your true friend.

During the recent global financial meltdown, which is yet to ease, many people who earlier had robust businesses suddenly found themselves vulnerable, unable to come to terms with the change in fortunes.

Some had no real help to fall back on, and that took a heavy toll on their businesses and personal lives. The suffering could have been avoided to a large extent if those people had some kind of connections at the datum level.

The need of nurturing local connections can hardly be understated. This doesn't take a lot of effort, but yes one should have the right mind to foster relationships.

For example, you as a professional web designer can think of helping entities like local charities, schools, NGOs, small businesses with your resources free or at a low cost as part of your relationship building.

When you do that, you can be assured of their help in your troubled times. Even if you are confident that no trouble will visit you ever, you can still benefit from the word-of-mouth publicity about your expertise and generosity.

8

RECOUNTING THE MAIN STEPS

There was a time when SEO only meant what is called 'onsite optimization'. All that mattered was tweaking the page title, the description, the headline(s), the keywords, the content, the image alt tags, and of course some incoming links.

Today SEO is not seen in isolation. It is just one portion in the bigger pie called online marketing. Maybe we should rather call it conversion.

For, at the end of the day, that is what matters irrespective of the type of website.

As the web is evolving more and more, it is becoming clear that the search engines may not be the only source of traffic to a website.

Social networking is an equally strong – some say stronger – sender of traffic, and so it makes sense to try out that.

Critics may say that the traffic from search engines are more committed than those from social networks, and consequently are more amenable to conversion.

This is true to a big extent, and so for small websites search engine optimization remains and shall remain the must-do effort to attract, retain, and convert visitors.

In this chapter we will look into some of the main steps for SEO that will have strong bearing on the success of a website in the long run.

Where to Begin

I endorse the view that SEO, over the years, has become somewhat complex. This I feel is inevitable because of the millions of websites coming online every day, each of them vying for attention.

At times it may seem difficult to decide which actions need to be prioritized.

The point I wish to make is that SEO is complex in the sense that you have many things on your plate to cater to, compared to what you would have done a few years back.

But certainly – and this is important to understand – SEO is not difficult to do.

I always maintain that SEO is about using your common sense, though many experts routinely term it as either a science or an art. It's neither, may I repeat.

SEO is about doing things I have explained in the earlier chapters regularly, without pause or ponder.

This point about regularity of doing certain things is missed by many. The other point they miss is that for new websites the effect of SEO, if done well, is not instantaneous and can be felt only after some time.

Given the wide scope of SEO activities, it is perhaps normal to feel overwhelmed, which is why it is always a good idea to divide the works in small modules and spread them uniformly over a period of time, say a week.

The same works are then repeated in the next week, then next to next, and so the cycle continues.

In my opinion, a large number of people take their websites lightly. They do not do sufficient groundwork and start a website like the drop of a hat.

This to my understanding is because the entry barrier to start a website is very low. A common thinking is perhaps that if a website fails, it is okay. One can always start another website.

On the contrary, if you take your website as a serious venture, and have thought out how you want to proceed, there is less reason to worry.

In this case you'll have a plan to work on, and if something goes wrong, you can always fall back on another course of action.

Based on my experience, I advocate the following 4 steps to start a website and make it successful. Of these, the preparatory works are usually not repetitive.

You do them once, and then proceed to the other steps.

The remaining three are however repetitive, and much of your success depends on how much time and effort you're able to spare for these 3 steps.

Let me briefly elaborate the 4 steps, following which I'll discuss a 6-month plan in the next section.

1. *Preparatory works*

   The commencement of a website is what involves the preparatory works. It all starts from the moment you decide to have a website for a business purpose. But let me come to the moment when you actually go for booking a domain name for your website.

   The steps for considering a website for your business, starting it, and building it brick-by-brick have been detailed in the Chapters 2 to 4. These are the tasks that form the bedrock on which will stand your web business.

2. *Contents*

   Since people primarily come to your site in search of some information, it goes without saying that you have to create and maintain a steady stream of relevant contents in your website. The contents can be text, image, audio and video. Creating contents is a regular exercise, and so as stated above, put aside fixed days in every week when you 'supply' contents to your website.

3. *Activities*

All actions outside of your website, but are geared to increase and enrich viewership to it, come under activities. These shall include social media updating, guest blogging, and all those described in the Chapter 7.

Activities, like contents, have to be done regularly. Earmark some days of every week to accomplish this task.

4. *Watch*

Under 'watch' comes the important task of measuring results. This is the only yardstick to understand what works and what doesn't for your website.

You need to install a traffic measurement tool like Google Analytics in all the web pages of your site. Google Analytics (covered in the next chapter) is of course much more than just measuring the flow of traffic to your site.

'Watch' is an important action and I feel this ought to be done daily even if only for say 5 minutes or so.

Making a 6-Month Plan

In business parlance, planning is a sacred activity. There are reasons. Human mind are programmed to work in a pattern.

People produce more output when they are able to work according to a plan. Planning produces predictability, an essential element in the jigsaw puzzle of productivity.

No surprise then that the progress of a website should also be planned in advance. This is not to suggest, as in case of large websites, that you need to have long sessions of discussions and deliberations, culminating in lengthy documents.

You can be brief, and your plan can very well be just a one-page detailing.

But planning you should be doing, not only to know what to do next, but also to be prepared to adequately meet unforeseen occurrences.

In the section, *Planning for Long Term* (Chapter 2; Figure 2.2), a tentative long-term plan has been shown.

This is a rough outline, but for the short term it is better to make a relatively detail plan so that you and your team members, if any, have a definite roadmap to follow.

Let me chalk out a typical 6-month plan for a small web business engaged in information sharing by blogging.

As is to be expected, I have taken the flow of traffic in terms of page-views as the benchmark index for planning subsequent steps.

Page-view is defined as the loading of a single HTML page of a website on to a browser. This can happen when someone clicks the link to the page in search result, from other page in the same or other website, or comes to the page directly by typing the URL of the page in the address bar of a browser.

The last one does not happen usually. Page view is an indicator of the popularity of a website and the pages within.

Internet marketers and advertisers consider the page-view figure of a website to decide whether or not to place ads in that website.

Okay now, let's look at the following 6-month plan for a newly-launched *content-based website*. The revenue model will be to earn mainly from renting out the spaces in web pages.

We will begin from the point where you have already decided the broad parameters of your proposed website, and are on the verge of booking a domain name for it.

Week 1-2

1. Buy a domain name, preferably having the main keyword in it.

2. Get a web host for your website.

3. Install WordPress (or other CMS), since you want an info-blog.

4. Decide the web design from a free/paid WordPress theme.

5. Decide the layout of the homepage and other static pages that can be the same as the WordPress theme. You can make the homepage slightly different even while keeping the same look and feel as the WordPress theme.

6. Write the stuff in the homepage as needed, stressing on the main keyword of your web business.

7. Submit your website to Google Places[8.1], and install the free Google Analytics code so that it appears in all the pages to come in your website (covered in next sections).

Week 3 Onward

Provided you've the basic structure of the website (see Structuring Your Website, Chapter 2) in place, the main job will be to build the contents. For a website to succeed, the need of relevant content will never end.

As stated earlier, the content can be in one or more of the 4 types – text, image, audio and video. Of them, text is essential, but only text is dull, boring, and uninspiring. And so it needs to be peppered with images, and audio and video, if conditions permit.

The points to remember while creating contents are briefly as under (see the sections *Making Content Easy to Read*, and *Creating Contents That Work* in Chapter 4, and also whole of Chapter 5, *Why Content Matters & How*):

1. The writing must offer something of value to the average readers. How-to articles, lists, tips, and suchlike are all-time favorites.

2. Internal linking from one article to another within your site is absolutely essential. The more you do, the better it is for your website in the long term. You may consider including relevant keyword or its variation in the anchor text.

3. To the extent feasible, weave each article around one or two keyword phrases that are relevant for your site.

Week 15 / 24 Articles Posted

Taking a modest 2 articles per week, let's assume you have penned 24 articles by the end of 15th week. Any visitor who comes to your site now will have a fair idea of what your site is about.

Also you may expect Google having indexed some of the article pages, if not all of them.

By this time you should start some off-site activities aimed at garnering links to your website as well as spreading your expertise on the topic of your website.

These will, as detailed in Chapter 7, include writing in other web publications, revving up Facebook profile, guest blogging, participating in forums, and so on.

In each case you have to do in a way that it helps your website. At the same time your effort should not look too obvious.

The visitors don't like hard pitching, and may in fact move off if you cannot tone down your approach.

Start watching the web analytics figures to get the early signals of source of traffic and the keywords the visitors are using to come to your site.

If you are following these steps copybook-style, and yes if your website covers a popular niche, and your choice of keywords is reasonably competitive, then there is a good chance that the page-views to your site on a monthly basis will notch upward of 300 if not more.

Though 300 is too small a figure as yet to come to a conclusion, it can however be indicative of the visitors' interest in your website, especially if it shows a rising trend.

Week 21 / Page-views Upward Of 1000

Certain factors that play important role in fast rise in page-views are as under:

1. Understanding the target market and ability to direct your effort toward it

2. Demand of your niche topic and availability of good quality supply in the target market

3. Your reputation in the niche…if you are well known in your niche subject, chance is very high that you'll get visitors pretty quickly.

4.   Your influence in your chosen social media circle. If you already have, for example, a good number of Facebook fans, your site will get visitors from the word go.

5.   Availability of email subscribers to a previous blog of yours. When you announce a new site to them, and if it is relevant to the earlier one, you get guaranteed visitors right from the beginning.

I have listed 5 criteria above, but there can be several others that can quickly get visitors to your site.

It is important to remember though that you have to maintain a healthy flow of relevant contents to have the early visitors stick to your site in search of more information.

When the flow of traffic and content occur in tandem, you may expect a surge in visitors flocking to your site in a short time, maybe in just 4 to 6 months or even less.

Week 24 / Page-views Upward Of 5000

I may be a little fast in predicting the page-views to an average website that does not have the advantages mentioned above. If however this does happen and you find that both the page-views and the pages per visit are rising fast, it's time for you to look at various ways to start earning from your site.

You may be offering an e-product for sale, which can be yours or an affiliate's. You can also earn from ads in your website by either renting out space or by clicks that the ads generate.

In the initial stage you'll have to place ads on your own volition, and earn after they are clicked by the visitors.

As your site keeps on improving the page-views, a time will come when interested advertisers will approach you for placing their ads in your site.

When this happens, you know you can now charge the advertisers for renting out space in your site irrespective of whether their ads receive any click-through.

This marks the beginning of earning good sum of money from your site. As you put in more efforts, the page-views increase, and the earnings too increase in tandem.

Page-views Upward Of 30000

Okay, I've made a big jump. But as your site consistently clocks in more than say 30K page-views and has an increasing trend, the time is ripe for starting sponsorship of products.

This is a good idea especially if the returning visitors constitute 20-25% of the total, because this means there is a loyal group of visitors who come often to your site. Watching the pages per visit also figure in this regard.

Week 30

In your eagerness to start and improve earnings from your site, don't lose sight of the number one priority – that of continuing to add relevant contents to your site.

The reason I reiterate this point once again is that after 6 months you will have a good idea about what is working well in your site and what is not.

The analytics data will give you a couple of vital information among a whole lot. You will know which keywords are bringing the maximum visitors, and which pages are seen the most.

You will also know which sites are sending you traffic and how much.

Among the referral sites that send you traffic, pay close attention to the top ones, and explore how you can further add or enrich your presence in those sites.

The keywords data may reveal a lot of other variations which you haven't thought of. These are the ones that you'll now use to write more articles.

Submit Website to Google Places

What was earlier Google's Local Business Center was changed to Google Places in April 2010. With this the concept of local search has firmly come to occupy the center-stage.

Once listed, a local business can be easily traced with the help of Google Maps.

The service is free, and in fact any business even without a website can avail it.

The following image (Figure 8.1) shows a typical listing of businesses (highlighted in red) for the geographical location of Gurgaon, Delhi in India.

Figure 8.1

Some of the important features of Google Places are as under:

1. Any business irrespective of size can be listed.

2. Information like address, phone number, photos, videos, car parking availability, and even special promos can be added to the listing.

3. Having a website is not mandatory.

4. Google confirms each listing by calling at the phone number given or by sending postcard at the given address. This is done so that only authorized owner of the business can add or alter the listing.

5. Google+ Local[8.2] is another product that helps users discover and share places.

Signing up for Google Places[8.1] is not difficult, and should be done even as your website is shaping up. Check out this PDF pullout[8.3] for more information.

Also read Google Places Cheat Sheet[8.4], a concise but helpful booklet.

Using Google Analytics to Study Traffic

One of the first things to do in your website is to install the free Google Analytics code[8.5].

It's a great tool that gives you deep insights into the flow of traffic to your website and their behavior while they are in your site.

Google Analytics, earlier known as the Urchin software which Google acquired in early 2005, is a must-use tool both for the fact that is free and also because it offers in-depth analyses of your website traffic.

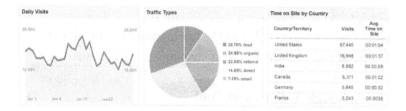

Figure 8.2

Some of the broad traffic indicators that you will get to know over a chosen period of time are as under (see the image above, Figure 8.2):

1. Number of visits, pageviews, pages per visit, percentage new visits, average time spent in the site, and bounce rate (the last one indicates how quick a visitor leaves the site; the lower the better)

2. How many pageviews of which pages and percentage of the total, how much traffic from which search engine, which referrals and direct arrivals.

3. Keywords used by visitors for arriving and percentage of the total.

4. Top landing and exit pages, top content by title, in-page analytics like which portion of the page receiving how many clicks, and so on.

If you are using AdWords campaign, you can interweave it with Google Analytics to analyze how your campaign is working, and the changes you should bring about for more conversions.

If you run AdSense ads in your website you can combine the account with Google Analytics to find out which pages are getting you more clicks on the AdSense ads.

As your site gets old it will be fascinating to study how the traffic to your website has been changing over the time.

Using Google Webmasters Tool

This is yet another very useful free tool from Google that helps you to properly run your website.

Dashboard

Search queries

Query	Impressions	Clicks
powerpoint 2010	5,400	46
thank you animation for powerpoint	2,900	22
google audio player	390	16
amazing powerpoint presentations	320	12
jquery catalog	210	46
powerpoint 2010 animation	140	16
powerpoint 2010 animations	140	16
jquery zoom image on mouseover	28	12

Nov 30, 2010 to Dec 30, 2010

More »

Links to your site

Domains	Total links
youtube.com	49
ajaxphotogallery.com	41
epochdvd.com	35
javascriptdatepicker.com	23
querylightbox.com	21

Figure 8.3

Let me quote from Google Webmasters Tools[8.6] how you can benefit by using it:

1. You can know how Google crawls and indexes your site and

learn about specific problems Google is having accessing it so that you can rectify them.

2. View, classify, and download comprehensive data about internal and external links to your site with new link reporting tools. Find out which Google search queries drive traffic to your site, and see exactly how users arrive there.

To understand the utility of Google Webmasters Tool, take a look at the image above (Figure 8.3) which is a portion of the dashboard page for one of my websites.

I can at a glance know the top search queries that fetched traffic to my site between Nov 30 and Dec 30, 2010.

The second table gives the total links from different domains that are pointing to my site. In each case the link *More >>* shows detailed results for that parameter.

Apart from the search queries and incoming links, the webmaster tools give some other vital information, one of which is the data on Internal Links.

As pointed out in the section, *Internal Links between Pages in a Website* (Chapter 4), Google places lots of weightage on the importance of internal links between pages of your website.

There are other information that can be had by using the tool.

For example, it diagnoses the different crawl errors like 'page not found', and for you as the website owner this is a great help to correct the mistakes if any.

Like Google Analytics, it is free to use Google Webmasters Tools. After you sign up with an account you'll be asked to verify that you are the owner of the site.

Once that is done, you have to indicate to Google which pages you want tracked. If you're operating a blog, simply give the feed URL and you're done.

It's a good idea then to visit the webmaster tools page for your website time and again to find out what Google feels about your website.

Installing SEO Book Toolbar

There are many free SEO tools available on the web that help you to glean important information about other websites, like the key-phrases they use, the incoming links to those sites, the overall traffic flow to those sites, and so on.

None, according to me, is as helpful and elaborate as the SEO Toolbar for Firefox[8.7] offered free by SEO Book. It can be installed only in Firefox browser[8.8] which too is free to use.

You have to set up a free SEO Book account to start using the toolbar.

This is a breeze, and once the toolbar is up there on your Firefox browser use it for access to a vast range of information (see image below taken from SEO Book site[8.9], Figure 8.4).

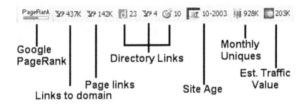

Figure 8.4

For a new website owner, such heavy information load may not mean much in the beginning.

But as time passes and your website gets more and more traffic, you'll be inclined to know more about other websites vis-à-vis yours to understand how your site is faring in the web marketplace.

Keeping Abreast of What Is New

Nothing is perhaps more effective than knowing the latest happenings around you. This may seem a bit overwhelming at times, but it surely keeps you in the loop on the face of fast-changing web scenario.

This book aims to teach you the basics of SEO and how you can easily do it yourself for your website. It is possible though that your main business is something else, and not about SEO or web marketing and your interest in studying this book is only to boost your SEO prospects.

With that in view, let me mention some steps below for you to remain abreast of the latest on the web in the field of web marketing and SEO.

1. Google Alerts[8.10] -
   You can set up alerts in Google for any search term, and let Google email you all the new information on the web for those terms. The search term can be your name, your website name, your main keywords, your competition's website name, or anything else. There is no limit to the number of alerts you set.

2. Google Video On YouTube[8.11] -
   Subscribe to Google's YouTube channel to receive whenever new news videos are released by the search giant. This simply lets you know something Google wants to tell all at the same time when everyone is getting to know.

3. comScore[8.12], Hitwise[8.13], and Nielsen[8.14] are some of the major sources of digital marketing metrics that give early information on major developments.

4. Subscribe to the RSS feeds of some major websites. These will include SitePoint[8.15], Search Engine Watch[8.16], SEO Theory[8.17], High Rankings[8.18], and Search Engine Land[8.19].

Learning from Experience

Learning remains incomplete unless you experience it by actually doing it. Experimental learning, to quote from Wikipedia[8.20], is the process of making meaning from direct experience.

An example of experiential learning is going to the zoo and learning through observation and interaction with the zoo environment, as opposed to reading about animals from a book. Thus, one makes discoveries and experiments with knowledge firsthand, instead of hearing or reading about others' experiences.

Putting it in a different way, experiential learning is learning through reflection on doing, which is often contrasted with rote or didactic learning.

This aspect is important in the case of practicing search engine optimization or SEO. Why?

As pointed out before, SEO today is more about how Google considers your website and the pages in your website to be important for any given set of keywords.

There is no science here really (except the proprietary mathematical algorithm used by Google), and there is no art also.

The only thing that matters is doing different things in a constant effort to try and rank higher in the search results. Add to this the fact that the web world is constantly changing, and new priorities and technologies are coming to the fore every other day.

It is therefore essential that as a website owner, eager to benefit from high search rankings, you need to dirty your hands in SEO.

When you do that you'll discover many small nuggets of value that have not been told to you.

An example is that of this A/B split test case study[8.21] that doubled the conversion rate by simply shifting an online form from below to one side of the webpage.

Consider the small experiences you come across to be your most valuable learning because you learnt them by actually doing what you are told to do.

The bottomline is simple. Search engines are man-made things and are susceptible to change listings whenever the people concerned feel the need to do so.

Thus, to be a gainer in the SEO game, you have to get down to the field and start playing it earnestly.

You Cannot Do Everything

By now you may have guessed that you may not be able to cater to all the aspects of SEO for your website all by yourself. After all for many of you SEO is one part of business marketing, and there are other parts of your business to look after.

Small businesses are prone to bear the brunt of slackening SEO efforts due to lack of sufficient manpower. Then again, the people you need to work for you have to understand the SEO concept well and know how it can be properly applied to your site.

Usually, the planning part of your website does not need many people. If you have grasped the concept well, you may be able to start your website and take it to the point where it has the foundation of say 20-25 articles and has been given the direction to proceed in the future.

The first sign of trouble becomes apparent when you need to ensure there is a constant flow of contents to your site, and also take care of vital works like link building, guest blogging, and so on.

This is the time when you need someone to help you in your works, and the best way to go about is to outsource the work you need done.

There is no dearth of freelancers who cater to all kinds of web-related works. Some of the renowned ones to search for freelancers are Freelancer[8.22], oDesk[8.23], Elance[8.24], PeoplePerHour[8.25], and Fiverr[8.26].

When you outsource works, keep in mind some important points as under:

1. You may not outsource all the works at a time. Identify the main work your site needs and decide how much of that you can do yourself. And then outsource the rest. For example, if content creation is the main work (I think it is) and you find you can write only 30% of your need, outsource the balance 70% of the writing needs.

2. Decide upon a monthly budget you can spare. This is important because you may not perhaps see any immediate tangible gains by spending on outsourcing.

3. Do not engage a freelancer for a long time. Give works in stages even though your need is for the long term. This is so because in many cases the freelancer, when assured of your work, may himself outsource it to someone else, thereby possibly affecting the quality.

4. For content writing works you have to be alert against the

chance of plagiarizing. Make this very clear that you have zero tolerance against any kind of plagiarizing. Remember many writers do clever plagiarizing by copying only few lines from different sites and then join them together.

So, to find out their trick, pick up a full line or a paragraph and search it in Google.

5. If your budget permits, get 3 to 4 content writers to work for you. Mention their names and brief bio at the end of respective articles, and also in a separate page like 'Who writes for us'.

   This sends a good signal to the visitors that your site is important and has many contributors from across the world.

6. Lastly, take a little time of yours and read the famous best-selling book, The 4-Hour Workweek[8.27] by Timothy Ferriss. This will unveil the steps on how to outsource your life to overseas virtual assistants for $5 per hour and do whatever you want.

Plan Ahead & Grow

Ok, I've at last reached the end section of my book. There are lists of valuable resources after this, but they are only lists, aren't they?

I select the topic, Plan Ahead & Grow, deliberately. I feel there can be no better parting wish to my readers than telling them to make a plan and stick to it to grow.

Over the years that I've been engaged in several web activities I've found planning to be of paramount importance. Planning gives direction, but more importantly, it cuts down the time to complete a work.

I can list several advantages to the credit of planning, but the following few are indeed important:

1. Planning involves engagement of mind before actually doing a work. It provokes you to think positively about how to take up and complete a work.

2. Planning means commitment to the work on hand. It helps you breaking the work into small elements that are manageable for completion within stipulated time.
   It also binds you into finding resources for those elements that need outside help.

3. Planning lets you find alternatives and make course corrections should anything go awry. This step is not considered essential by many. As a result, when something goes wrong, they don't have any alternate plans to fall back on.

4. Contrary to point 3, if the business grows faster than you imagined, planning helps you to take the full advantage of it. In absence of suitable planning, your business may altogether miss the golden opportunity of fast growth.

5. When planning is done in consultations with your colleagues, everyone in your company knows what is expected of her/him. This way the flow of work becomes smooth, and the overall output can be maintained along expected lines.

With these words, and wishing a prosperous business to all of my readers, let me conclude this book.

You are most welcome to contact me for anything you want to let me know.

The contact details are given at the beginning of this book.

Here it's again, team@hubskills.com.

Lastly if you have liked reading this book, please tell about it to your friends, relatives, colleagues and anyone else you like to. And do please write a review in Amazon to let me know your experience about this book.

Finally, don't forget the free lifetime enrollment to my video course on SEO Best Practices for Beginners to Start Web Business, coming next.

BONUS
FREE ENROLLMENT TO MY VIDEO COURSE

S trange it may sound, but in my fairly long coaching experience I have seen that people learn things better when they watch a video.

This could be because video encapsulates all the 4 information gathering medium, namely text, image, audio, and video.

In case of learning a concept as evolving as search engine optimization, it is no wonder that video plays a vital role in the proper explanation of why and how SEO matters to small businesses.

I am happy to offer my video training course, SEO Best Practices For Beginners To Start Web Business, free of cost to all the readers of this book.

The course has 30 videos that lucidly explain the vital concepts of SEO. Viewers will have the opportunity to download the video transcripts to understand the lessons better.

The advantage of my video course is that once enrolled, readers will enjoy lifetime access to it with no cancellation whatsoever.

What's more, viewers will get to ask me any questions they want clarified.

To get the course for free, go to the following URL at Udemy.Com, and then use the coupon code, SPECIAL-OFFER.

- https://www.udemy.com/seo-foundation-course-for-starting-web-business/

Alternatively, copy the URL given below and paste it on your browser to get the course for free:

- https://www.udemy.com/seo-foundation-course-for-starting-web-business/?couponCode=SPECIAL-OFFER

You have to open an account at Udemy.Com, but you can also use your Facebook account to take the course.

My best wishes to you all!

BIBLIOGRAPHY

To write this book I have taken help from a wide gamut of inputs in different websites and publications. Throughout this book I have specifically mentioned those references in superscripts, and here in the bibliography I'm going to mention the URLs of those resources.

This I hope will help the readers to know more about the topics and assist them to take a wholesome look at SEO.

Chapter 1: Understanding Search Engines

1. How Internet Search Engines Work [http://computer.howstuffworks.com/internet/basics/search-engine1.htm]
2. Algorithms Rank Relevant Results Higher [http://www.google.com/competition/howgooglesearchworks.html#section1]
3. Google Algorithm Change History [http://moz.com/google-algorithm-change]
4. Mozcast [http://mozcast.com/]
5. Study Finds That Memory Works Differently in the Age of Google [http://news.columbia.edu/googlememory]
6. Google's Financial Results Q1-2013 [http://investor.google.com/earnings/2013/Q1_google_earnings_tab7.html]

Chapter 2: Planning SEO For Your Web Business

1. Business Models On The Web
    [http://digitalenterprise.org/models/models.html]
2. What is a Web Strategist? [http://www.web-strategist.com/blog/2008/05/17/what-is-a-web-strategist/]
3. Google's Quality Guidelines for Webmasters
    [https://support.google.com/webmasters/answer/35769?hl=en#3]
4. Study by Penn State University's IST Researchers on Classification of Web Searches
    [http://news.psu.edu/story/189289/2008/04/02/ist-researchers-classify-web-searches]
5. How to Name Your Business
    [http://www.sitepoint.com/how-to-name-your-business/]
6. Free WordPress Themes
    [http://wordpress.org/extend/themes/]
7. Google's Matt Cutts on Using WordPress
    [http://www.robsnell.com/matt-cutts-transcript.html]
8. WordPress Plugin Directory
    [http://wordpress.org/extend/plugins/]
9. Book: Why Most Small Businesses Don't Work and What to Do About It by Michael Gerber
    [http://www.amazon.com/gp/product/0887307280]

Chapter 3: Researching Keywords for Your Site

1. What History Tells Us About Facebook's Potential As Search Engine
    [http://searchenginewatch.com/article/2065524/What-History-Tells-us-About-Facebooks-Potential-as-a-Search-Engine-Part-1]
2. Words per search is increasing in US (graph)

[http://www.comscore.com/var/comscore/storage/images/
media/images/words-per-search/571505-1-eng-US/words-
per-search.gif]

3. The 20 Most Expensive Keywords in Google AdWords
   [http://www.wordstream.com/articles/most-expensive-
   keywords]

4. Can you give us an update on rankings for long-tail
   searches? (Google video)
   [http://www.youtube.com/watch?v=WJ6CtBmaIQM]

5. Wordtracker Keyword Research Tool
   [http://www.wordtracker.com/]

6. Market Samurai Keyword Analysis Tool
   [http://www.marketsamurai.com/]

7. Keyword Eye Visual Keyword & Competitor Tools
   [http://www.keywordeye.com/]

8. YouTube Statistics
   [http://www.youtube.com/yt/press/statistics.html]

9. Google AdWords Keyword Tool
   [https://adwords.google.com/select/KeywordToolExternal]

10. AdWords Help Articles
    [https://support.google.com/adwords]

11. Google Instant
    [http://www.google.com/insidesearch/features/instant/abou
    t.html]

12. Bing Ads Intelligence, BAI
    [http://advertise.bingads.microsoft.com/en-us/bing-ads-
    intelligence]

13. YouTube Keyword Suggestion Tool
    [https://www.youtube.com/keyword_tool]

14. Incremental Search
    [http://en.wikipedia.org/wiki/Incremental_search]

15. Keyword Tool Dominator
    [http://www.keywordtooldominator.com/k/amazon-

keyword-tool/]
16. FreshKey Keyword Analyzer
Software[http://freshkey.com/]
17. Twitter Search [http://search.twitter.com/]
18. hashtags.org [http://www.hashtags.org]
19. Hashtags: helping you find interesting Tweets
[http://support.twitter.com/articles/49309-what-are-
hashtags-symbols]
20. Übersuggest Keyword Suggestion Tool
[http://ubersuggest.org/]
21. Wordtracker [http://www.wordtracker.com/]
22. Market Samurai [http://www.marketsamurai.com/]
23. WordStream [http://www.wordstream.com/]
24. Keyword Discovery [http://www.keyworddiscovery.com/]
25. SEO Book Keyword Suggestion Tool
[http://tools.seobook.com/keyword-tools/seobook/]

Chapter 4: Knowing The SEO Basics

1. 10 things we know to be true
[http://www.google.com/about/company/philosophy/]
2. Google's User Experience Principles
[http://www.cxacademy.org/googles-user-experience-
principles.html]
3. You Aren't Average [http://www.seobook.com/you-arent-
average]
4. 8 Things Website Owners Can Learn From Gordon Ramsay
[http://searchenginewatch.com/article/2065944/8-Things-
Website-Owners-Can-Learn-From-Gordon-Ramsay]
5. Each SBI! owner below has achieved life-changing goals
[http://ctpm.sitesell.com/priority.html]
6. Title Tag and Meta Description Length for Google, Yahoo,
Bing & Ask [http://www.sagerock.com/blog/title-tag-meta-

description-length/]

7. Google does not use the keywords meta tag in web ranking [http://googlewebmastercentral.blogspot.com/2009/09/goo gle-does-not-use-keywords-meta-tag.html]

8. Headings and Subheadings http://writing.colostate.edu/guides/page.cfm?pageid=567]

9. Article by Sage Lewis [http://www.clickz.com/clickz/column/2137991/the-beginning-a-very-good-place-start]

10. Article by Karon Thackston [http://www.wordtracker.com/academy/seo-copy]

11. Changing URLs [http://www.searchengineguide.com/jill-whalen/changing-urls.php]

12. "Straight from Google: What You Need to Know" [http://www.robsnell.com/matt-cutts-transcript.html]

13. SEO vs. SEF [http://www.clickz.com/clickz/column/1721773/seo-vs-sef]

14. Let Google find, index, and rank your site [http://www.google.com/support/webmasters/bin/answer.p y?answer=35769]

15. 10 Common Content Usability Mistakes on a Web Page [http://www.thomsonchemmanoor.com/10-common-content-usability-mistakes-on-a-web-page.html]

16. You Don't Deserve #1 by Todd Friesen [http://www.mediapost.com/publications/article/113024/#a xzz2]

17. SEO Advice: Writing useful articles that readers will love [http://www.mattcutts.com/blog/seo-advice-writing-useful-articles-that-readers-will-love/]

18. It Isn't Good Content Unless it's SEO'd Content [http://www.searchengineguide.com/stoney-degeyter/it-isnt-good-content-unless-its-seod-con.php]

19. Link Counter Tool

[http://linkcounter.submitexpress.com/index.php]
20. Google on Duplicate Content
    [http://www.google.com/support/webmasters/bin/answer.p
    y?hl=en&answer=66359]
21. Similar Page Checker [http://www.webconfs.com/similar-
    page-checker.php]
22. Comparing Duplicate Content (between 2 pages)
    [http://www.webseoanalytics.com/free/seo-tools/duplicate-
    content-checker.php]
23. Copyscape Plagiarism Checker
    [http://www.copyscape.com/]
24. Plagiarism Checker [http://www.articlechecker.com/]
25. Eric Enge Interviews Matt Cutts
    [http://www.stonetemple.com/articles/interview-matt-
    cutts-012510.shtml]

Chapter 5: Why Content Matters & How

1. Debate – Can you judge a book by its cover?
   [http://www.debate.org/opinions/can-you-judge-a-book-
   by-its-cover]
2. Only 2 out of 10 people read an entire copy
   [http://www.copyblogger.com/magnetic-headlines/]
3. Headlines, Intuit Community
   [http://community.intuit.com/library/articles/headlines]
4. Will You Be E-Mailing This Column? It's Awesome
   [http://www.nytimes.com/2010/02/09/science/09tier.html]
5. Are Your Titles Irresistibly Click-worthy & Viral?
   [http://moz.com/blog/are-your-titles-irresistibly-click-
   worthy-viral]
6. How To Write Near-Perfect Headlines In Minutes
   [http://www.wordtracker.com/attachments/PerfecttHeadlin
   es-final-part-1a.pdf]

7. Generating ideas of content types to engage, by Danyl Bosomworth [http://www.smartinsights.com/content-management/content-marketing-strategy/the-content-marketing-matrix-new-infographic/]

8. Secrets to Writing Engaging Titles & Content for SEO [http://searchenginewatch.com/article/2235149/Secrets-to-Writing-Engaging-Titles-Content-for-SEO]

9. Article by Jeff Bullas [http://www.jeffbullas.com/2013/01/10/20-ideas-for-content-that-people-love-to-share-on-social-media/]

10. E-book by Jon Morrow [http://headlinehacks.com/]

11. Gadwin PrintScreen [http://www.gadwin.com/printscreen/]

12. Evernote Skitch [http://evernote.com/skitch/]

13. IrfanView [http://www.irfanview.com/]

14. Flickr photos with Creative Commons Attribution License [http://www.flickr.com/creativecommons/by-2.0/]

15. morgueFile free photos [http://morguefile.com/archive]

16. CSS3 Button Generator [http://css3button.net/67371]

17. CSS Button Designer [http://www.cssbuttondesigner.com/]

18. CSS Button Generator [http://www.cssbuttongenerator.com/]

19. Google Charts [https://developers.google.com/chart/interactive/docs/gallery]

20. easel.ly [http://www.easel.ly/]

21. Creately [http://creately.com/]

22. Visual.ly [http://create.visual.ly/]

23. Piktochart [http://piktochart.com/]

24. infogr.am [http://infogr.am/]

25. Audacity [http://audacity.sourceforge.net/]

26. Free royalty-free music [http://hubskills.com/free-royalty-free-music-for-your-video/]

27. WP Audio Player [http://wordpress.org/plugins/wp-audio-

player/]
28. oEmbed HTML5 audio
[http://wordpress.org/plugins/oembed-html5-audio/]
29. How to Make Sleek Professional Video With PowerPoint
[https://www.udemy.com/powerpoint-video-training/]

Chapter 6: Advanced SEO Considerations

1. Jill Whalen on Alt Text
    [http://www.highrankings.com/forum/index.php/topic/431
    76-image-link-vs-text-link/]
2. Text near image is important
    [http://www.seobook.com/archives/001602.shtml#8627]
3. Eyetrack III –Larger online images hold the eye longer than
    smaller images
    [http://www.poynter.org/uncategorized/24963/eyetrack-iii-
    what-news-websites-look-like-through-readers-eyes/]
4. What Is PageRank?
    [http://en.wikipedia.org/wiki/PageRank#Description]
5. Pictorial illustration of PageRank
    [http://upload.wikimedia.org/wikipedia/commons/thumb/f
    /fb/PageRanks-Example.svg/400px-PageRanks-
    Example.svg.png]
6. Google uses site speed in web search ranking
    [http://googlewebmastercentral.blogspot.com/2010/04/usin
    g-site-speed-in-web-search-ranking.html]
7. Google Research: Speed Matters
    [http://googleresearch.blogspot.com/2009/06/speed-
    matters.html]
8. Best Practices For Speeding Up Your Website
    [http://developer.yahoo.com/performance/rules.html]
9. Yahoo! YSlow [http://developer.yahoo.com/yslow/]
10. Yahoo! YSlow as Firefox Add-on

[https://addons.mozilla.org/en-US/firefox/addon/5369/]
11. Google Code: Page Speed Downloads
    [http://code.google.com/speed/page-speed/download.html]
12. WebPagetest [http://www.webpagetest.org/]
13. Pingdom Tools [http://tools.pingdom.com/fpt/]
14. Sandbox Effect or Google Penalty
    [http://en.wikipedia.org/wiki/Sandbox_effect]
15. The Age of a Domain Name
    [http://www.webconfs.com/age-of-domain-and-serps-article-6.php]
16. Domain Age Tool [http://www.webconfs.com/domain-age.php]

Chapter 7: Getting Links by Reaching Out

1. Google's advice
   [https://support.google.com/webmasters/answer/34432?hl=en]
2. Google' change of stance on links
   [https://twitter.com/Baeumlisberger/status/347099333428121602/photo/1]
3. How to Fix Broken Link Graph
   [http://www.seobook.com/how-fix-broken-link-graph]
4. Link Building is not Illegal
   [http://www.stonetemple.com/link-building-is-not-illegal-or-bad/]
5. Interview with Fraser Cain
   [http://searchenginewatch.com/article/2187666/From-0-to-3-Million-Monthly-Visitors-Learn-One-Mans-Proven-Strategy]
6. Hubpages [http://hubpages.com/]
7. Squidoo [http://www.squidoo.com/]
8. rel="nofollow" explained

[https://support.google.com/webmasters/answer/96569?hl=en]

9. Mashable [http://mashable.com/submit/]
10. ClickZ [http://www.clickz.com/contact-us?contact_forms[entity_attribute]=Become%20a%20Columnist]
11. SitePoint [http://www.sitepoint.com/write-for-us/]
12. BloggingPro [http://www.bloggingpro.com/archives/2010/06/29/guest-posting-on-bloggingpro/]
13. Smashing Magazine [http://www.smashingmagazine.com/how-to-become-a-smashing-magazine-author/]
14. Guest Blogging (membership course) [http://guestblogging.com/]
15. My Blog Guest [http://myblogguest.com/]
16. Stop using article directories [http://searchenginewatch.com/article/2242706/10-Common-Link-Building-Problems]
17. Best Article Submission Sites For Link Building [http://www.wordstream.com/blog/ws/2009/07/29/best-article-submission-sites-link-building]
18. Leave Comments on Other Blogs [http://www.problogger.net/archives/2009/04/25/leave-comments-on-other-blogs/]
19. What is Internet Forum? [http://en.wikipedia.org/wiki/Internet_forum]
20. How to Use Forums To Drive Hundreds of Thousands of Readers to Your Blog [http://www.problogger.net/archives/2008/10/20/how-to-use-forums-to-drive-hundreds-of-thousand-of-readers-to-your-blog/]
21. PRWeb [http://www.prweb.com/]

22. URLwire [http://www.urlwire.com/]
23. Free Press Release [http://www.free-press-release.com/]
24. PRLog [http://www.prlog.org/]
25. Press Release Writing Tips from the New York Times [http://www.cbsnews.com/8301-505125_162-29540250/press-release-writing-tips-from-the-new-york-times/]
26. 5 Killer Press Release Tips For Small Businesses [http://smallbiztrends.com/2009/10/five-killer-press-release-tips-for-small-businesses.html]
27. Stand Out: The Power Of The Press Release [http://www.problogger.net/archives/2008/02/29/stand-out-the-power-of-the-press-release/]
28. Learn making video with PowerPoint [https://www.udemy.com/powerpoint-video-training/]
29. The Database of Intentions Is Far Larger Than I Thought [http://battellemedia.com/archives/2010/03/the_database_of_intentions_is_far_larger_than_i_thought]
30. Facebook Passes Google In "Time Spent" [http://searchengineland.com/facebook-passes-google-in-time-spent-who-should-care-50263]
31. 10 web sites where surfers spend the most time [http://www.usatoday.com/story/money/business/2013/03/09/10-web-sites-most-visited/1970835/]
32. Hitwise figures of top 10 social media websites [http://www.experian.com/hitwise/online-trends-social-media.html]
33. Facebook vs Google: No Contest [http://www.seobook.com/facebook-vs-google-no-contest]
34. Facebook Marketing: Ultimate Guide [http://moz.com/blog/facebook-marketing-ultimate-guide]
35. Twitter statistics [http://www.statisticbrain.com/twitter-statistics/]

36. How to Use Twitter for Business
[http://www.pcmag.com/article2/0,2817,2383408,00.asp]

Chapter 8: Recounting the Main Steps

1. Google Places [https://support.google.com/places/]
2. Google+ Local
[https://support.google.com/plus/answer/2531255]
3. Help for Google Places
[http://static.googleusercontent.com/external_content/untr
usted_dlcp/www.google.com/en//help/hc/images/Google_P
laces_OneSheeter.pdf]
4. Google Places Cheat Sheet
[http://btsmallbusinessoptimization.com/wp-
content/uploads/2011/03/Google-Places-Cheat-Sheet.pdf]
5. Google Analytics
[http://www.google.com/analytics/index.html]
6. Google Webmasters Tools
[https://www.google.com/webmasters/tools/]
7. SEO Toolbar for Firefox [http://tools.seobook.com/seo-
toolbar]
8. Download Firefox [http://www.mozilla.com/en-
US/firefox/]
9. SEO Toolbar image [http://tools.seobook.com/seo-
toolbar/data-overview.png]
10. Google Alerts [http://www.google.com/alerts]
11. Google Video on YouTube
[http://www.youtube.com/user/Google]
12. comScore [http://www.comscore.com/]
13. Hitwise [http://www.experian.com/hitwise/]
14. Nielsen [http://www.nielsen.com/us/en/about-us.html]
15. SitePoint [http://www.sitepoint.com/]
16. Search Engine Watch [http://searchenginewatch.com/]

17. SEO Theory [http://www.seo-theory.com/]
18. High Rankings [http://www.highrankings.com/]
19. Search Engine Land [http://searchengineland.com/]
20. Experimental Learning in Wikipedia
    [http://en.wikipedia.org/wiki/Experiential_learning]
21. An A/B split test case study: How to double your
    conversion rate [http://www.smartcompany.com.au/online-
    sales/20101210-an-a-b-split-test-case-study-how-to-
    double-your-conversion-rate.html]
22. Freelancer [http://www.freelancer.com/]
23. oDesk [http://www.odesk.com/]
24. Elance [http://www.elance.com/p/landing/buyer.html]
25. PeoplePerHour.Com [http://www.peopleperhour.com/]
26. Fiverr [http://fiverr.com/]
27. The 4-Hour Workweek by Timothy Ferriss
    [http://www.amazon.com/gp/product/0307465357]

RECOMMENDED READS

Though I have covered this book in fair details, you may still like opinion by other authors. Read the following books as further reference:

1. The Comic Guide to SEO by Amit Bhawnani
    http://www.amazon.com/The-Comic-Guide-SEO-ebook/dp/B006TYW95A

2. SEO 2013 & Beyond :: Search engine optimization will never be the same again by Dr. Andy Williams
    http://www.amazon.com/SEO-2013-Beyond-optimization-ebook/dp/B0099RKXE8

3. SEO Made Simple - Search Engine Optimization Strategies for Dominating the World's Largest Search Engine by Michael Fleischner
    http://www.amazon.com/SEO-Made-Simple-Edition-ebook/dp/B00AW18ITM

4. SEO for WordPress: How To Get Your Website on Page #1 of Google...Fast! by Kent Mauresmo & Anastasiya Petrova
    http://www.amazon.com/SEO-WordPress-Website-Google-Fast-Volume/dp/1481948377

5. The 4-Hour Workweek: Escape 9-5, Live Anywhere, and Join the New Rich by Timothy Ferriss
    http://www.amazon.com/gp/product/0307465357

PARTHA BHATTACHARYA

ABOUT THE AUTHOR

Partha Bhattacharya is the founder of HubSkills.Com, and a do-it-yourself web entrepreneur with more than 10 years' experience in different web technologies. He offers e-learning courses in his website, and also on Learnable.Com and Udemy.Com, the premier online education portals.

Partha is a writer, a blogger, a video maker, and a coach cum consultant, helping entrepreneurs starting e-business.

To know more about Partha's works and how he can help you, visit the website HubSkills.Com, the YouTube Channel, and the Facebook page.

http://hubskills.com
http://www.youtube.com/hubskills
https://www.facebook.com/HubSkills

To engage Partha for any coaching, consultancy or speaking responsibility, contact him at:

Email: team@hubskills.com
Skype ID: kirebaba